D1547851

SOULFUL LEADERSHIP

A Spiritual Path to Health,
Wealth, and Love

Mark Porteous

Published by
Hybrid Global Publishing
301 E 57th Street
4th Floor
New York, NY 10022

Manufactured in the United States of America, or in the United Kingdom when distributed elsewhere.

Porteous, Mark
Soulful Leadership: A Spiritual Path to Health, Wealth and Love
LCCN: 2020919891
     ISBN: 978-1-937055-03-5
eBook: 978-1-937055-04-2

Cover design by: Jonathan Pleska
Copyediting by: Claudia Volkman
Interior design by: Suba Murugan
Author photo by: Deborah M Kulig Letourneau

https://markporteous.com

CONTENTS

INTRODUCTION

Mark Porteous

We live in a unique time in human history. The choices we make individually and collectively over the next decade will determine the direction of humanity's path. We are entering a new era in the story of humankind that penetrates every aspect of life, including how we serve in business, politics, organizations, and families.

"A New Way of Being" is emerging that supports the good of the whole. Visionary pioneers like you are leading the way. As a Soulful Leader, YOU are a beacon of light and a powerful force in the Universe!

To be a powerful force of good, you need to be CONNECTED—connected to who you are at soul level, connected to your Divine Purpose, and connected to your Soul Tribe.

Together, we are shifting human consciousness from our current state of "fear and the illusion-of-separation" to our natural state of "love and deep connection."

To make this critical shift, what is needed MOST right now is Soulful Leadership.

Soulful Leadership is recognizing that you are a Divine Being who has chosen the "human experience" for a reason and then living in alignment with that knowledge by making conscious choices for the highest good. Your leadership is expressed in how you show up—as a person, for your family, in your community, and through your work.

And how, you might ask, will Soulful Leadership help you attain optimized health, abundant wealth, and deeply loving relationships in your life, as the title of this book suggests?

My promise to you is that as you read these personal stories, it will become abundanly clear how you can live an extraordinary life while transforming the lives of others.

Soulful Leadership: A Spiritual Path to Health, Wealth, and Love is designed to guide you through the Evolutionary Path of the Soul-Connected Entrepreneur and to provide valuable wisdom about life's most meaningful questions: "Who am I?", "Why am I here?", and "How do I thrive in my Divine Purpose?"

Every chapter tells a powerful story by an author who demonstrates Soulful Leadership in the world. Each story offers valuable insights and practices you can integrate into your life now. These stories weave together like a fine tapestry, illustrating the Quest of the Soulful Leader.

The people you are here to serve are Heroes. Their experience with you is much like the Hero's Journey. The Hero is "called" and ventures out into the unknown on a mystical quest. There he or she discovers unimaginable challenges and obstacles. The Hero also meets a guide with a map and special gifts to support the Hero in overcoming his or her challenges and obstacles.

We are the Guides. We hold the maps and the tools needed by the Heroes we each serve. Your "Customer Journey" is a powerful tool for your clients. It's also very helpful in providing clarity for your Dream Team AND for attracting affiliate ambassadors to share your work with their audiences.

This collaborative project also serves as an example of how to develop your own Soul Affiliate Alliances to amplify your impact in the world and demonstrates what they can look like in the New Paradigm of Business and Life.

In addition to the treasures provided in each chapter, the authors have also provided special gifts to support your Hero's Journey. You can learn more about these authors and download their valuable tools at no cost by visiting our website, www.SoulfulLeadershipBook.com.

Part One

CONNECTING TO WHO YOU REALLY ARE

Who you are at the deepest innate level of your human nature is the most important element in your life. Who you are at this deep level is your most important contribution to this world.

I guarantee that adapting this perspective WILL change your life.

Your journey as a Soulful Leader begins and evolves through personal awareness. The more you learn about who you really are and how to optimize your presence in this world, the greater will be your success, happiness, and life effectiveness.

You've been on a lifelong trek of self-discovery, learning more and more about who you are so you can BE all you came here to be and DO all you came here to do.

To discover why we are here, first we need to better understand what we are. I refer to "we" as both a collective and as each of us individually. Collectively, we are a family, a community, a nationality, a race, and a species. Individually, we are composed of three very unique components: Body, Mind, and Spirit.

Our bodies are physical objects made of matter. Matter is anything that has mass and occupies volume. Albert Einstein's Theory of Relativity led to many amazing discoveries, including the relationship between mass and energy. Einstein explained that mass and energy are transmutable. We are familiar with the equation E= mc2. In physics, mass–energy equivalence is the concept that the mass of a body is a measure of its energy content. All physical objects are made of energy; therefore, we, our physical bodies, are made of energy. This is a scientific truth.

"If you want to know the answers to the universe, think in terms of Energy, Vibration, and Frequency." —Nicola Tesla

Because we are self-aware, we realize that we are more than our bodies. Psychology, the study of the mind, was considered to be a branch of philosophy until 1879, when it was developed as an independent scientific discipline in Germany and the United States. The mind is so mysterious that it was considered to be philosophical, not scientific. Just as we continue to learn about the physical world, our understanding of the human mind continues to expand. Understanding the power of conscious and subconscious thought is an important part of understanding who and what we are.

Theories can be debated in both physics and psychology. Both subjects are now accepted as science. The controversy gets far more intense when we discuss the theories, or even the existence, of spirit. If you think the mind is a mystery, the spirit may seem absolutely magical.

Abraham Maslow talks about your innate, unchanging core values being the essence of who you really are. In the Grand Perspective, you are a Divine Being who is one with Source and all that is. Your mind is the bridge between body and spirit and the gateway to personal transformation.

Tapping into Source for Inner Guidance is the single most important skill that you can master to navigate through life.

At your inner core, you are directly connected to Source and to All That Is. This is your true "Being."

When you start with "being," ALL your "doing" becomes inspired action. One ounce of "inspired action" can be more effective than one hundred pounds of "raw action." You will get incredible results when your "doing" directly reflects your "being."

Imagine for just a moment if all you had to DO to make a bigger impact and a greater income was to BE more of who you REALLY are so that every action you take is inspired, joyful, and in your highest good.

The stories included in Part One will provide you with tools, practices, and perspectives to help you discover more of your magnificence and will help you train yourself to hear the whispers of your inner guidance and take inspired action so you can avoid the alternative, a two-by-four to the head.

1. REVOLUTIONARY AGREEMENTS FOR SOULFUL LEADERSHIP

Marian Head

Are you aware of the agreements you have with your business associates, clients, and loved ones? Do your agreements support you in being the fullest expression of your authentic self?

We make many agreements during our lives—spoken and unspoken, conscious and unconscious. As business leaders, we enter into contractual agreements, employment agreements, and nondisclosure agreements. Written agreements help us to clarify our expectations, and this is good. Yet as I have grown and evolved, I have come to know that the most powerful agreements are those agreements I have with myself. Every action I take, every response I make, comes from these agreements.

Thirty-five years ago, I began living from a specific set of agreements with myself. At that time, my husband was president of the Win/Win Business Forum, a weekly meeting of spiritually minded business owners. He invited some of these business leaders to our home to explore a question together: "How can we support one another to live our highest values in every aspect of our lives, and especially in our work where we spend most of our time?"

At that very first gathering in June 1985, we meditated together, drew insights from the Field, and began developing a set of agreements to guide us on our path. That group decided to meet again one month later. In addition to fun and expansive practices that fed our bodies, minds, and spirits, we shared how the agreements were positively affecting our lives and the lives of those with whom we worked and lived.

Without any obligation or membership, this forum, dubbed the "Geneva Group," continued meeting for a full day every month—for the next twenty years! We began each gathering by reading and discussing the agreements. As we evolved, the agreements also evolved. Fifteen years after our first gathering, I shared the essence of those agreements with the world, calling them "Revolutionary Agreements."

What's So Revolutionary about These Agreements?

These Agreements are *revolutionary* in that they have the potential to transform the prevailing paradigm of negativity to one of positivity and possibility. At a personal level, they can transform stress and struggle into freedom and joy.

These Agreements are also *evolutionary*. According to Barbara Marx Hubbard, creator of the Foundation for Conscious Evolution:

Although they may appear simple at first glance, the Revolutionary Agreements hold the keys to transformation. Practicing the Agreements gently moves us from Ego to Essence. This evolves us into the deeply loving people we were designed to be by the Impulse of Creation.

People who practice these Agreements find support for being their best selves, staying centered during times of crisis, resolving conflicts with greater ease, and bringing out the best in others. What distinguishes Revolutionary Agreements from contractual agreements is that first and foremost, they are agreements with *ourselves*.

HEALTH, WEALTH, AND LOVE

The Revolutionary Agreements have become my guide to living my life's purpose: *to be Love in Action*. For myself and many others, the application of these Agreements has led to outrageous financial success in businesses that fulfill us.

As a member of the "million-dollar club" for a global wellness corporation, I was invited to attend an extravagant forum on a beautiful tropical island. C-suite executives met with the top sales leaders of over 250,000 world-wide reps. At one point the meeting turned contentious. My business partner and I gently offered the Agreements as a possible way through our combative stance.

"Marian's leadership, holding fast to the principles of these Agreements, trans-formed interpersonal and organizational struggles of 'I'm right—you're wrong' into genuine, joyful collaboration, ultimately creating 'we' out of 'us and them,'" said an executive consultant present at that forum.

The ability to effectively use the Revolutionary Agreements does not require my presence. A consultant to a Fortune 100 company recommended the Revolutionary Agreements to its stressed-out director of Systems and Opera-tions. Seven months later, the director wrote: "To say that this core organi-zation has turned itself around would be an understatement." Perhaps my favorite part of his report was: "I can say that I am in love again with my career and assert that the Agreements are the best tools for stress reduction I have ever found."

Transforming stress to love? I knew I had to share these Agreements with other soulful leaders! The more "Love in Action," the better.

I decided to write a book about the Revolutionary Agreements in order to extend their powerful results into the world. I condensed what was then sixteen wordy (albeit inspiring) Geneva Group agreements to twelve easily digestible chunks.

Those twelve settled into three groups, representing what I call three "pillars" of a good life:

- Truth—being the truth of who you are, your authentic self
- Acceptance—accepting others for who they are in this present moment
- Gratitude—feeling and expressing appreciation for the precious gift of life and all it has to offer

Each pillar is comprised of four Agreements that provide a structure for being Love in Action. I'll comment on one Agreement in each of the pillars. I invite you to thoughtfully consider which Agreement in each pillar might have the most positive effect on your life if you were to practice it regularly.

TRUTH
I agree to live my mission.

The cornerstone of a soulful leader's success is her or his passion, aka "calling" or mission. This Agreement is not about *achieving* our mission, but rather about *living its essence*. In that way, we can enjoy a fulfilled life now instead of waiting for some future day's achievement to reward us.

What is the essence of your mission? How do you or could you live its essence now?

I agree to speak my truth with compassion.
I agree to look within when I react.
I agree to keep doing what works and change what doesn't.

Which of the above four Truth Agreements would make the greatest positive impact on your life if you were to practice it consistently?

ACCEPTANCE
I agree to resolve conflicts directly.

Nothing sucks our energy more than an unresolved conflict. If you are ever burdened by one, consider when the burden is the greatest: when you are with the person with whom you are resolving the conflict, or in the days, weeks, months (and sometimes years) leading up to addressing it?

When we apply this agreement to resolve a conflict as soon as possible (and with only the person with whom we can resolve it), our energy is released to soar to infinitely creative and productive heights.

I agree to listen with my heart.
I agree to respect our differences.
I agree to honor our choices.

Which of these four Acceptance Agreements would most serve you and those you serve if you were to practice it regularly?

GRATITUDE
I agree to look for blessings in disguise.

Have you ever dealt with something difficult, maybe even traumatic, that you later saw as a blessing in your life? When we practice this agreement, we can transform worry, anger, and blame (including ourselves) in an instant. Embodying this agreement is having faith that Love is present, even if the proof is not apparent.

When we go through hard times together as a team, family, nation, or world, soulful leadership is especially important. As we model love and compassion, faith and optimism, we can energetically transform personal and collective stress into greater peace and joy.

I agree to give and receive thanks.
I agree to see the best in myself and others.
I agree to lighten up!

Which of the four Gratitude Agreements is most important for you to practice in order to fully enjoy the health, wealth, and love you deserve?

The One Master Agreement

Practicing these agreements eventually leads to the One Master Agreement. This Agreement has the greatest impact on our leadership today and our legacy forever. While no single phrase can adequately capture its essence, I offer this:

I agree to be my Self.

Why the capital "S" in "Self"? To remind us that we emanate from a Divine source. To honor our life as a gift from our Creator, and to remember that what we do with it is a gift to all Creation.

To know that when we embody Love in Action, we are fulfilling our soul's purpose.

I encourage you to allow these Revolutionary Agreements to be one of your cherished guides to Soulful Leadership. While they are first and foremost Agreements with yourself, they will have a profound influence on your relationships, which are the bedrock for your success in every aspect of your life.

This practice is so profoundly powerful in its simplicity that I am declaring the Revolutionary Agreements as the Constitution for my business. They support me with a structure for "being the change I want to see in the world."
—Mark Porteous, 2016

Marian Head is the award-winning author of three books, including *Revolutionary Agreements: A Personal Path to Peace on Earth*. Whether building her multimillion-dollar global wellness business, consulting to Fortune 100 companies, facilitating gatherings of world leaders, or parenting her child, she credits the Revolutionary Agreements as the practice most responsible for her achievements.

www.RevolutionaryAgreements.com

2. DO YOU KNOW YOUR MIND TYPE?

Hubert Lee and Ridgely Goldsborough

Why do we suffer a mid-life crisis? Or an identity crisis? Or any personal crisis? Why do people in seemingly stable circumstances melt down for no apparent reason?

Do adverse winds suddenly blow in with such force as to thrust your lifeboat into a perfect storm? Of course not. It takes a gradual build up, a seedling of doubt that grows over time, tiny shoots of disappointment and regret that crack the surface while they simultaneously sink their roots.

When you don't know your **WHY**—your purpose and meaning—you become vulnerable, like a house built on sand or on a shallow foundation. Anything can sway you.

Since the beginning of man, the quest for understanding **WHY** we exist has led us into momentous directions—the drive for conquest and war, the establishment of philosophies and religion, the crusade for moral mandates that shape our behavior.

No matter where you find yourself on the spectrum, two fundamental questions will plague you until resolved: *WHY am I here? WHO am I?* No one can answer these questions for you. Only you know. Or at least, some part of you knows—AND THAT'S THE CHALLENGE.

The answer lies deep beneath the surface, not easily accessible, in the very fabric of your being, forged so early on that you don't even perceive it as it takes control of your future and becomes the programming that guides every action you take.

We call it your *MIND TYPE*, the embodiment of your belief system. It manifests continually through your thoughts, words, and deeds. It explains in full living color **WHY** you do everything that you do. Where does it come from?

Your primary and most basic instinct as a human being is survival. Your secondary driving desire is the need for love and companionship. *Your Mind Type stems from both*, at the most primitive level.

When you crave milk as an infant, what do you do? Scream. And what happens? Someone brings you milk—which helps you "survive." On a feeling level, screaming equals survival.

When you wake up in the middle of the night scared and alone, what do you do? Scream. Someone comes and comforts you. On a feeling level, screaming equals love and companionship.

On both counts, screaming equals success.

From that point forward, any time you have a need or a want, you scream. If it worked before, it will work again—until it doesn't.

If your caretakers stop responding to your cries, your needs and wants nonetheless continue. If crying no longer gets a response, you try something different, a new behavior or course of action.

When you find one that works, you repeat it. And then you repeat it again. Like pieces of code wired into your personal programming, each successful act leaves a mental imprint. That worked—do it again. This didn't—go back to plan A.

Think of every successful act as a slim wire filament. One single filament has limited strength.

As you bind it with a second one and then a third and a thousand more after that, suddenly you build a wire cable capable of holding a massive bridge—certainly strong enough to control your belief system. In short order your coding sets. The proven pattern of behavior becomes your driver, how you survive and succeed in life.

This coding shapes, molds, and forges your *Mind Type*, **WHY** you think the way you think, **WHY** you speak the way you speak, **WHY** you do literally everything that you do.

Your *Mind Type* quite literally takes over the governance of your existence. It is the engine that drives your decision making based on early programming that met your most fundamental needs of survival and love.

Your *Mind Type* will never change nor turn off. It is as much a part of you as your physical body.

Whether you know your *Mind Type* or you don't, it still runs you. Like the law of gravity, it affects every choice you make—whether you understand it or not, agree with it or not, or have any knowledge of it at all.

When you embrace your *Mind Type*, your existence makes more sense. Your motivations flow seamlessly and elegantly. You gain immense clarity about who you are and how you view the world and operate in it. It empowers and guides you.

When you live it, you acquire immense power—the power to be yourself in all of your glory, to find where you fit and share that with the world. You answer the question: "WHO are YOU?"

When you discover your *Mind Type*, you understand your WHY.

You are a Superhero. Yes, YOU! Through your *Mind Type*, you have unique Superpowers. Each *Mind Type* also has its own unrivaled Kryptonite—a flaw or weakness to which that *Mind Type* is susceptible.

In each case the Kryptonite is directly related to the Superpower, the perfect antithesis to the Superpower's greatest strength. When you fully understand both, you can maximize your power and neutralize the Kryptonite—you can bring forth your potential, your talent, your gifts.

There are seven Mind Types: The Giver, The Connector, The Problem Solver, The Innovator, The Perfectionist, The Rebel, and The Master. *What's yours?*

Although you will always have a primary *Mind Type*, you can put on the Superhero cape of any of the others whenever you need to and tap into their Superpowers as well. A fully realized leader who understands his or her own *Mind Type* and how to use it can both recognize and appreciate the *Mind Type* of others and will temporarily discard their own Superhero cape in favor of another to accomplish a goal—with the understanding that they will naturally default back into their own identity with ease.

When you flick a switch and the light comes on, the room looks different in an instant. A cave that has been dark for ten thousand years brightens with a single candle. Discovering your *Mind Type* feels just like that—a burst of instant clarity.

We exist, decide, select, move, shift, interpret, enjoy, and agonize based on our *Mind Type*. It affects EVERYTHING. *Don't you want to know what yours is?*

What a mess we endure as humans! Few of us truly have any clue what drives us, what guides us, or what influences our decisions. What if we could change all of that? Future-cast for a second. You fully get who you are. You understand yourself. Your relationship craziness actually makes sense—because you perceive your part in it.

Your business and career foibles become more obvious and comprehensible because you understand what part you've played in each challenge. You know what to do next time, how to tap your Superpower for maximum success.

Your *Mind Type* gives you great clarity about yourself. Your *Mind Type* allows you to unleash your full power. Your *Mind Type* complements other *Mind Types* who can multiply your strengths.

Discovering your *Mind Type* can be likened to the Hero's Journey. To survive and thrive early on, without conscious realization you have experimented with multiple behaviors and failed many times—maybe even most of the time—and then you found something that worked, something that resonated, something that both "felt" right and yielded the desired result. Like donning a Superhero's cape, you exert your newfound "Superpower" through the same behavior. It sticks with you.

You are Clark Kent. You step into the phone booth and come out as Superman. Except that this time, you wear your cape all the time. The only need for a phone booth is to step in and change capes—to don the powers of another *Mind Type* while you need them.

When you honor yourself and other *Mind Types*, you gain immense power—the power that comes from respect and humility, from understanding who you are, and from a desire to use your power for good. Be yourself in all of your fully expressed splendor. Our belief is that we can change the world one empowered *Mind Type* at a time.

All that's left is to discover YOURS. Your future awaits!

With his "Master" Mind Type, **Hubert Lee** believes in digging deep into every nook and cranny of topics such as digital marketing and social media. As a Problem Solver, **Ridgely Goldsborough** believes in making sense out of things for the benefit of all involved—always! Together they have helped thousands of people discover their Mind Types.

www.MindTypes.com

3. A CASE OF MISTAKEN IDENTITY

Lisa Engles-Witter

To say that we live in unprecedented and turbulent times is nothing new; it's something you've most likely heard, thought, and experienced. The big question on everyone's mind is "What's next?" Global pandemic, civil unrest, climate change, economic collapse—what's next? Every day we're hit with *another* piece of shocking news. Confidence is dwindling as uncertainty mounts.

How did we get here? How is it that we find ourselves in arguably the worst global crisis we've ever faced? But first we need to consider the idea that everything we're experiencing right now is a symptom, a consequence of past actions. The crisis we're currently facing and the tremendous suffering that has resulted both personally and collectively is caused by our conscious and unconscious actions.

The Law of Cause and Effect: Every Action Has a Consequence

It's a simple enough idea, right? For every action, there's an effect or a consequence. In Eastern spiritual tradition, it's called the Law of Karma. Our actions are inseparable from and interdependent with other people. It's impossible for the action of one person to not affect another person in their sphere of influence and ripple outward across time and space, creating a complex web of causes and conditions that result in an inconceivable number of situations, circumstances, and events. Some of these we think of as "good" or pleasurable, and others we think of as "bad" or painful.

And right now, we're experiencing a Mount Everest of consequences at the collective level. If what we're experiencing right now—the pain and suffering, the global crisis—is the result of our past actions, then we need to ask ourselves another question: What *type* of actions have led us to our current situation? Now, you might be thinking, *Hey, I didn't create this situation!* They *did.* T*hey* meaning the politicians, the government, the other party, the lobbyists, the 1 percent who own 99 percent of the world's wealth, the "bad guys." *They, not me* is precisely the *type* of thinking that got us into this situation, because thinking is an action. And ***misinformed thinking leads to misinformed action*** which leads to . . . climate change, civil unrest, economic breakdowns, global pandemics, and every type of injustice and inequity.

The solution, of course, is to take responsibility for our misinformed actions (and we've all taken misinformed actions) and the hurt our actions have caused others and ourselves. We need to recognize that our actions have far-reaching effects, sometimes years, decades, or even lifetimes into the future. Case in point: In 1864 the Thirteenth Amendment was added to the United States Bill of Rights, as a "constitutional guarantee" of "perpetual freedom." However, the way it was written, argued then-Massachusetts Senator Charles Sumner, was simply a deceptive way to reestablish slavery by another name. This created America's carceral state and the disproportionate number of Black people who are incarcerated today, over 150 years later.

Our misinformed actions, however, can be traced back to something more fundamental.

So now we arrive at the point of this chapter: The reason why we're experiencing social and global crises right now is because of a case of mistaken identity. We've mistaken ourselves (and others) to be something other than who we really are. Our minds and hearts have been confused, making us believe that we are our religious and political preferences, our race, color, creed, and gender. We've been confused into thinking and believing that we are our social status, our personality, and our intellect. *This case of mistaken identity has caused us to take misinformed actions* in the name of protecting something that we are not. Now is the time for us to reclaim our True Identity as a reflection of the One Infinite Love Intelligence. Through this reclamation process, we will come to realize that it's not our body or our beliefs we need to protect with our actions—but rather our one human race and the Great Mother Gaia that provides us with life.

Answering the Question "Who am I?"

"Who am I?" and "What's my purpose?" are perennial questions that man has been trying to answer for millennia. Knowing the answer to these questions gives our life meaning and direction. But we must begin with the first question, "Who am I?" In answering that question, the answer to the second question, "What's my purpose?" becomes self-evident.

In Yoga philosophy, practitioners are encouraged not to think about or ponder these questions; rather, they are given time-proven practices that gradually open them to the realization—*through direct experience*—of the answer. So, it's in that vein that I offer the following and encourage you to **experience** the Truth of who you are versus understanding it conceptually. The danger in not knowing who you really are, as a felt experience, is that you will continue to live a life in reaction to all the causes and conditions of your past (karma) and continue to take misinformed action which will sooner or later lead to the experience of suffering.

There are two answers to the question, "Who am I?" If you only know one answer, then you have a half-understanding of who you really are. To discover both answers and have a full understanding of who you really are, Eastern Spiritual Tradition asks us to consider that there are two levels of Reality. The first level of Reality is referred to as Absolute Reality. Absolute Reality is the undifferentiated, unmanifested Spirit, also known as *Satchitananda* in Yoga tradition. *Satchitananda* is the description of Spirit: *Sat* = Ever-Existing; *Chit* = Ever-Conscious; and *Ananda*

= Ever-New Joy/Bliss. The second level of Reality is Relative Reality. It consists of the manifest world and everything in it. Both levels of Reality—the non-dual and the dual—co-exist at all times. However, most of the time, most people are only aware of Relative Reality, and so they experience their Self primarily (if not solely) from that level of awareness even though there is another experience of Self available to them.

I Am a True Self

From the level of awareness of Absolute Reality, we discover that the answer to the question "Who am I?" is "I am a True Self." The term *true self* often gets used interchangeably with *authentic self*, especially among personal growth coaches and therapists who are using these terms from the perspective of Relative Reality, not Absolute Reality. However, the distinction is critical. The True Self is that aspect of you which is a pure reflection of the One Divine Love Intelligence—Spirit. The True Self exists as the ever-present, ever-aware witness of all that you experience. Again, a conceptual understanding of the True Self will get you across town, but not through it. It's necessary to have a *direct experience* of your True Self if you want to take your ego-consciousness back to the Divine Source at the core of your being where all sense of separateness disappears. It's from this knowing of Self that you also begin to perceive the True Self of all other beings on this planet.

There is a classic pointing-out instruction referred to as self-inquiry in Advaita Vedanta that, when practiced with discipline and thoughtfulness, will eventually bring the practitioner into a direct experience or knowledge of the True Self. I highly recommend watching any of Swami Sarvapriyananda's YouTube videos on self-inquiry if you're interested in hearing a spiritual master describe the practice.

The practice itself consists of four steps. First, the practitioner discerns between the seer and the seen, discriminating between objects in the external world and the one who is seeing those objects. Second, the practitioner discerns between the seer and the senses, which perceive the external world. Third, the practitioner discriminates between the seer and the mind—the mind being all internal thoughts and feelings. And finally, the practitioner makes the distinction between the seer and the ego, the "I" that's identified with the body, emotions, thoughts, and mental constructs. This practice brings one to the realization that whatever one can perceive as an object externally or internally is not the Self. The True Self is the eternal subject, which witnesses all but Itself, which cannot be witnessed.

While all of this may sound abstract, once you experience your Self in this way, you will open to the realization that there is only one True Self, which exists in all humans. The statement "We're all one" will take on new meaning, and the inevitable result is that your actions will reflect this knowledge.

I Am a Unique Self

When we operate from an awareness of Self in Relative Reality at our highest level of consciousness, we experience our Self as a unique expression of the Divine that lives in us, through us, and as us. The term *Unique Self*, first coined by Marc Gafni in his book *Your Unique Self*, is commonly used to describe this experience.

A frequently used example in Eastern Spiritual Tradition is the ocean and the wave: The wave is part of the ocean, but not the ocean itself. Waves come in all shapes and sizes, and eventually their "life" comes to an end as they hit the shore and are consumed back into the ocean. In the same way, we are each unique expressions of Spirit. When Spirit manifests in Relative Reality, it manifests as diversity (uniqueness). No two things are identical in manifest reality—including plants, animals, and humans. We are each a Unique Self. As Gafni beautifully puts it, when you experience yourself as a unique self, "you understand that your uniqueness is the highest expression of God looking out from behind your eyes and taking in your uniquely gorgeous perspective and insight."[1]

We all experience our uniqueness as a deep truth. The teachings of Yoga tell us that while it's important to deconstruct the separate self and realize our True Self,

---

[1] Marc Gafni, *Your Unique Self: The Radical Path to Personal Enlightenment* (Tucson, Ariz.: Integral Publishers, 2012) 57.

we can never escape our diversity . . . our uniqueness. In realizing our uniqueness, we discover that we are not replaceable; there never was, is, or will be anyone who can fill our shoes. Realizing our uniqueness dissolves any desire to be like someone else or to have what someone else has.

Becoming Agents of Personal and Social Change by Claiming Our True Identity

So, while we can't change our past actions or the consequences of those actions, we can change the course of humanity and become agents of personal and social change by taking informed action today. The road to healing the divide in humanity and the destruction to the planet begins with knowing the answer to the question "Who am I?" as a felt experience.

When we know the truth of who we really are, both as a True Self and as a Unique Self, we are given the gift of perceiving the true nature of all other beings. When we're able to perceive the true nature of others, compassion, loving-kindness, and forgiveness become the basis of all our actions.

Lisa Engles-Witter is a psycho-spiritual coach and counselor and the creator of the Karma Clearing Process™. Her work draws from timeless and proven principles and practices based in Yoga tradition. She has worked side by side with some of today's most influential luminaries and thought leaders in evolutionary spirituality, most notably the late Barbara Marx Hubbard.

www.lisaengles.com

4. EMOTIONAL MASTERY: CHANGE *CAN* BE EASY

Andrea Isaacs

Tell me, what is it you plan to do with your one wild and precious life?
—Mary Oliver

He's offstage in his "ready to go" spot stage left. He's poised, focused, and alert. He's standing tall, his shoulders wide. He hears his introduction and bounds up the steps to the stage.

He confidently strides to center stage, turns to fully face the audience while connecting both feet firmly on the ground. He inhales fully and deeply as he looks to his right, his left, and back to center, taking in the whole audience. Everyone is looking at him.

He breaks into an ear-to-ear smile that cracks his face wide open. His smile gets even bigger—it's as if his heart cracks open and smiles too.

As he continues to look out into the audience, he makes everyone feel that he's looking right into their eyes and seeing into their hearts.

Sitting in the audience, I am bursting with pride! It wasn't that long ago that I had done coaching sessions for Mark because he was nervous about pulling off his first three-day event. The closer the day of the event came, the more afraid he was that he just wasn't enough, that he'd be seen as a "fraud."

He felt his old football shoulder pads on his shoulders again, working double-duty to protect him just in case someone saw through his veneer.

There was so much at stake.

He knew he had a mission and a drive that fueled him every day. Yet the idea of being seen and judged fueled his fear of failure.

But he HAD to do it. There was no way he wanted a job working for anyone else. Being in the shackles of someone else's dream was *not* an option.

Driven? Yes. Scared? Yes.

This kind of moment is a fork in the road. This is a "choice point."

In preparing for his event, Mark faced two choices:

- Put a stake in the ground for his mission and take inspired action toward realizing his dreams and goals.
- Procrastinate, not get the support he needed, be fearful of judgment, resist because it felt too big, and then unintentionally hold back and not fulfill his mission.

To those who have made the first choice, applaud yourselves!

To those who have made the unintentional choice to hold back, you probably think that change is difficult. And there's good reason for this.

Every one of your thoughts, feelings, or actions has a neural pathway.

Those thoughts, feelings, and actions that you've repeated most often strengthen those particular neural pathways, just as you strengthen your muscles by doing repetitions.

This is great if the patterns you're repeating, training, and strengthening are patterns of confidence, courage, patience, or speaking up for yourself—of getting on stage and letting the world know your message!

However, if you repeat patterns that hold the fear of not being enough, fear that you're an imposter, or fear of criticism, you are holding yourself back from showing up as powerfully as you could. Life then becomes a struggle, and you won't make an impact.

When the Choice Point comes, you'll probably procrastinate, take the "automatic pilot" response you've done before even though you don't like it—for instance, playing small and not being seen—because the neural pathway for it is so strong.

Mark came to me as a client to help him be a more magnetic, powerful leader. He had strong neural pathways well-trained over a lifetime of hearing and believing that he wasn't enough and that he had no value, and he was afraid of being seen as a fraud.

Together we created new neural pathways that gave him new options and changed him so that he was able to powerfully show up, stand in his value, embody his message, and speak with authority.

And you can create new neural pathways too!

After searching for answers to life's mysteries at the age of nineteen, I found a reason to be here, a reason that made life worth living, one that came with the commitment to live life to its fullest. I believe you're here for a reason too. The question is: Are you living it? If you are, great! You're probably living a meaningful, joyful life. If you're unclear about why you are here, though, it's likely that you want more meaning and more joy in your life.

Change *CAN* Be Easy!

When you know how to create new neural pathways, you can:

- be that next bigger, bolder version of yourself
- easily make empowering choices
- embody your message
- empower your voice
- make the impact you're here to make

After guiding Mark in this process, his fears subsided, and he was able to show up powerfully on stage and speak with authority.

I've guided clients around the world in this change process. Here's a brief exercise that will give you a sense of what can be possible.

Three Steps to Change

Step One: Notice Your Body

I'm going to invite you to notice and listen to your body. Imagine that your body is communicating to you like a TV or radio station that you can't quite hear, so you turn the volume up.

To turn up the volume on your "body channel," it's useful to repeat and exaggerate as much as you can. That's when you can start to sense and finally *hear* what your body is telling you.

Ask yourself: "What's the biggest thing holding me back from accomplishing my dream?"

Temporarily bypass your thinking mind. Notice the energy in your body as you imagine what's been holding you back.

When Mark did this exercise, he imagined the biggest blocks holding him back:

- He felt his football shoulder pads protecting him from criticism.
- The pads were heavy on his shoulders. His whole body felt heavy.
- He started to drop and slouch.
- His chest constricted, and it became hard to breathe.

Your response will be different. Whatever your response is, be aware of your body without judgment.

- **Notice it.** Does your body feel contracted, explosive, constrained, heavy, floating, gripping, distant, angry, etc.?
- **Allow it.** There's no "wrong" way to do this exercise. This is something your body wants you to know. Experience how it would feel if you DON'T go for your dream.
- **Turn up the volume.** Repeat and exaggerate this feeling in your body. Imagine feeling this all day. Do it again, and again, and again. Get a taste of what this would be like if you don't change it.

Step Two: What Would Your Body Prefer?
This may sound like a weird question, so again, temporarily bypass your thinking mind.

Ask your body this question:
"What would you prefer?" Whatever your response is, be aware of your body without judgment.

- **Notice it.** Notice the littlest movement in any body part.
- **Allow it.** There is no "wrong" way to do this exercise. This is something your body wants you to know. This is what it would feel and be like if you DID go for your dream.
- **Turn up the volume.** Whatever your body does, repeat and exaggerate *this* in your body. Do it again, and again, and again. Imagine feeling *this* all day.

In Mark's case:

- He threw off those shoulder pads.
- He started to walk and stomp, each step connecting more and more with the earth, each step more and more powerful.
- His chest expanded as he breathed in fully and deeply.
- His arms shot outward, extending into space.
- His whole body strengthened, rooted in the earth, and connected above.

Step Three: Anchor It

We anchor it by using a *mudra* (a gesture or body position, traditionally a prayer or meditation position) and a *mantra* (a word or phrase). These are Sanskrit words, both with the intention to create a particular inner state.

Anchor it in your body: your *mudra*. Gradually come to stillness in a body position that captures how you'd rather feel. This body position will become your *mudra*.

In Mark's case, his *mudra* became:

- Standing with both feet firmly anchored into the ground
- his spine long and his shoulders wide
- his arms shooting outward, extending into space

Anchor it in your mind: your *mantra*. Feeling this energy in your body; what does it say about you now? Complete this "I" statement: "I am ..."

In Mark's case, his *mantra* became:

I am a mountain of power.

When a *mantra* (phrase) is used with a *mudra* (body position) that holds the same intention, it is very powerful in instantly creating new neural pathways that change your brain, change the energy in your body, and change how you think, feel, and respond to life's challenges.

The next time you find yourself procrastinating or holding back, follow these three steps to change.

And then change *CAN* be easy!

And then you will be able to live your one wild, meaningful, precious, and joyful life.

THIS is emotional mastery!

Andrea Isaacs is the founder of the Isaacs Method for Emotional Mastery and creator of the EQ Quiz. As a speaker, trainer, and master of change, she has brought more meaning and joy to the lives of thousands of people around the world with her unique system that combines emotional intelligence, body wisdom, the Enneagram, and neuroscience.

www.Andrea-Isaacs.com

5. NOTE TO SELF: PAY ATTENTION TO YOUR INNER COMPASS

Ariela Sarai, MSW

"I knew I should have . . ." How many times have you said this to yourself? You have an inner voice that is always trying to guide you toward fulfilling your greatest dreams. It's like a compass set for your highest good, but you usually dismiss it. Wouldn't it be nice to consistently pay attention to that deep guidance within so you can stop regretting your decisions and create an extraordinary life?

Even if you have almost everything you want, you may still feel unfulfilled. Maybe you want to make a change but don't have a clear direction. You might feel disconnected from your purpose or from the people in your life. Maybe you're just living on autopilot. If you can relate to these, you have lost touch with your inner compass.

As a child I was taught to always be productive and positive. I didn't want to disappoint anyone, so whenever I was upset about something, I tuned out my emotions. My personal motto became *"Just deal with it."* I kept trying to meet people's expectations while suppressing my inner voice. Even when I faced major challenges, I didn't reveal what was happening to anyone. Throughout childhood my stuffed feelings kept intensifying. They turned into strong waves of anxiety and sadness. Still I brushed them off and continued to focus on excelling at my activities.

I was successful at building a life that looked good on the outside. As a young adult I traveled to India for over a year–first volunteering alongside Mother Teresa then studying Buddhism with Tibetan monks. I got two Ivy League degrees, became a psychotherapist, got married, and had a child. These were all incredibly meaningful, but I had become an expert at turning a blind eye to my personal struggles. I didn't recognize how depleted, confused, and unhappy I was.

Eventually I got divorced. As my world fell apart, I couldn't keep pretending any longer. I knew I had to stop rejecting my inner voice that was quietly illuminating my truth, my boundaries, and my deepest desires. I committed to listening to it and taking charge of my life.

Right after I made that decision, I found the support I needed to get real and reconnect with my true self. I was able to create a life I love both inside and out. Since then I have devoted myself to living in integrity, following my heart, and empowering others to be grounded and aware so they can truly flourish.

I'm going to share some discoveries about what gets us off-track and what we can do to reconnect with our inner guidance.

Five Habits That Lead to Regret

1. Tuning out

Tuning out your feelings may start as a coping strategy, but as you work on creating the life you want, it becomes a big obstacle. You stop being real. You were taught that you need to be positive and get rid of anything "negative." But when you put a lid on your feelings, they don't go away. They form internal landmines that can come out in spurts of anger, sadness, or over-reactivity. They continue to get louder until you pay attention to them.

Feelings carry a message that needs to be heard, not rejected. When you are honest about how you feel, you will know exactly where you stand. This self-awareness is the first step in reconnecting to your inner guidance. No matter what it is that you need to acknowledge, facing it will enable you to stay centered and grounded.

2. Pretending

When you pretend that you are fine for so long, you may lose your ability to tell the difference between your pretense and your intuition. That is because they are both talking to you! You have so many voices in your head that you don't know what to listen to. You become lost in a labyrinth of mixed messages.

When this happens, you can default into a trance-like state in which you just put up with things for years. You may stay in a toxic work environment, repeat the same frustrating patterns with your partner, or feel chronically overwhelmed without resolving the situation. There is usually a benefit you are getting, such as making money or avoiding conflict. You may not realize how much you are sacrificing in order to hold on to that benefit.

You CAN stop sleepwalking through life. You can learn to discern the difference between your higher guidance and your old agendas. When you do, you will stop doubting yourself and find the next step on your soul's path.

3. Being indecisive

Are you stuck on the fence, afraid to make the wrong decision about something? If so, the first step is to determine what type of pain you are experiencing.

There are two kinds of pain, and it is vital to know the difference:

1- The pain that is caused by something that is damaging
2- The pain that is caused by stretching out of your comfort zone

If you are exercising and something starts to hurt, first you need to determine whether the pain is due to an injury or caused by the process of building new muscles. If it is due to an injury, continuing to exercise will cause damage. If it comes from building new muscles, continuing to exercise will cause growth.

This also applies to emotional pain. If you feel stuck in a relationship, is it because it is destructive for you? Or is it because you are avoiding facing some issues that would come up no matter what relationship you were in?

It is important to determine what type of pain you are experiencing. Then you will know whether you need to end something or embrace a stretch. This will give you the courage to choose a direction and commit to it.

4. Not speaking up

You might be hesitant to speak up about what you really feel, see, or need. You assume that you are going to have to deal with people's reactions or unwanted consequences. This may or may not be true, but the idea can be enough to shut you down.

The problem is that when you don't *say* what you feel, you start to *show* what you feel in unhealthy ways. You can end up unconsciously sabotaging yourself to be heard instead of communicating. You may start telling yourself that if you suffer enough others will notice what they are doing to you. You may put in less effort at work to try to show that you don't agree with a new policy. You may employ the silent treatment with your partner to get your point across, but that just increases the separation that was upsetting you in the first place. These strategies only end up destroying your progress, peace, and well-being.

It requires exceptional self-honesty to admit that you might be doing these things. But you are not alone. This is more common than most people realize. When you really own what you want to say, you will find the courage to speak up. You will stop working against yourself. You will trust that saying the truth always leads you to greater opportunities for personal transformation and growth.

5. Hiding who you really are

When you disconnect from your inner voice, you also disconnect from your inspiration. You may hide the more vulnerable and creative aspects of yourself for fear of disapproval. It's human nature to want to fit in, but when you reject yourself in order to be accepted by your partner, family, or group, your life feels flat.

I have a mini Australian Shepherd. She twirls around and around every time she gets excited. It is an expression of pure joy and enthusiasm. When she was a puppy, the trainer asked me if I wanted to teach her to stop twirling. It took my breath away. I couldn't imagine training her to shut down her natural exuberance.

Have you been shutting down the things that light you up? You might want to make more time for your spiritual practice, play music, start a business, begin drawing again, or have a greater impact. Following your heart's unique impulses is what makes you feel vibrant and fully alive. When you value your own worth, you will welcome your authentic voice and will find a way to express it while connecting with people you love.

The Path to Extraordinary Living

"The heart is magnetic, silent, and still. Within the heart you will also find clarity, resolve, intent, respect and kindness." *Love Without End* by Glenda Green

Your divine guidance has always been there, even though it may have become a faint echo. Reconnecting with it is like plugging into a source of internal clarity and power. You are able to tap into your soul's vision and direction.

Listening to your divine guidance is the key to living an extraordinary life. You will consecrate your path and live with purpose, connection, and deep joy.

Tuning In: The Gift of Awareness

Here are some questions for reconnecting with your inner voice. When you answer them you will see that painful emotions become valuable messages, confusion is transformed into clarity, and you start to cultivate your home base within. I encourage you to be totally honest with yourself.

Tune in to your feelings:

What feelings have I been dismissing?
How do I feel right right now?
What feelings am I hiding?

Tune in to your life circumstances one at a time:

What have I been refusing to see?
How do I really feel about this circumstance?
What do I want to change about this circumstance?

Tune in to your decisions one at a time:

What harm is this situation causing, if any?
What stretch am I being called to make?
What am I avoiding?
What do I know that I am not acknowledging?
What is my next step in making this decision?

Tune in to what you need to say:

What do I want to say that I haven't said?
What am I trying to show instead of communicate?
What is my true intention for sharing what I want to say?

Tune in to your heart's desires:

What is truly important to me?
What dreams have I buried?

What do I love doing most?

What sides of myself would I love to express?

Deep, lasting fulfillment is possible when you honor your inner voice. If there is only one thing you remember from this chapter, let it be this: **Take the time to pay attention.** Pay attention to what you are feeling, to your circumstances, to your heart's desires, and to your divine guidance. When you do, you will rekindle your inspiration to live your most magnificent, authentic life.

Bio

Ariela Sarai, MSW, is passionate about helping people stop dismissing themselves so they can experience a whole new level of aliveness and creative power. With her remarkable ability to deeply listen, she has supported hundreds of people to reconnect with their inner compass and create the fulfillment they have been longing for.

www.ArielaSarai.com

6. TO ATTRACT ALL OF WHAT YOU WANT, KNOW ALL OF WHO YOU ARE

Nancy Benitez

The time had come. As I sat in the darkness of my closet with tears streaming down my face, I knew the decision to finally end my marriage would completely change the course of my life.

It had taken me five years to come to this decision, and it wasn't something I had taken lightly. Over the course of those years, I had allowed the essence of who I was and what I wanted as a woman to disappear. By my own doing, I had become the "yes" mom, wife, and friend. I said yes to everything and everyone else but me, and my needs, my health, and desires had become nonexistent. In my gut, I knew something had to change. I had to change, and so did my choices.

On the outside we had been the perfect couple. We had been together for seventeen years, married for thirteen. We had traveled the world, had the big house, the parties, the cars, the vacations, and a beautiful daughter who had been the main reason I had talked myself into staying.

I had supported his dreams and helped him reach his goals, but now the time had come to step into my own life purpose as the powerful individual I knew I was meant to be.

I had learned, loved, and experienced so much, and for that I was grateful, but I knew that staying would only keep me from becoming the woman I was meant to be physically, spiritually, and energetically.

I also knew that walking away from my relationship was only a small part of my expansion and growth. I knew that no matter where I went, I would take myself with me. That meant taking all of the sadness, anger, limiting beliefs, and the wounded parts of myself too.

In leaving my relationship, I wanted to learn how to love myself by myself—to grow, expand, heal, and fully step into creating my own happiness and my own wealth and abundant life. It was time to stop hiding, stop avoiding what my heart felt, stop making excuses, and begin finding worth and love inside myself.

I was ready to take the leap, so about a week after my encounter in my closet, we sat on the couch and began to talk. I was so nervous; my palms were sweaty, and there was a heaviness in my heart. I did not want to have this conversation, but I knew it was necessary.

He looked at me, and with a stoic look on his face, he asked, "Is our marriage over?" I courageously said, "Yes!"

To be honest, inside I was terrified. The decision I had just made meant that I was about to step out of everything that was familiar to me into the discomfort of being on my own again. Looking back, however, I was relieved and far more excited, ready, and curious to discover how it would all unfold. I looked at this as my opportunity to start over and ascend into love with myself.

I'm not going to lie, though. The two years that followed leaving my relationship and being a single mom by choice were full of many challenges and heartaches, especially when it came to our daughter and her understanding of what was happening. I was really grateful that her dad and I could communicate like kind, caring adults and had the opportunity to show our daughter that we could get along and co-parent.

There were many days when I wondered if I had made the right decision. I wondered if things would have gotten better had I stuck things out. Then there was the chatter, opinions, and comments of well-intentioned friends and family that made it even more of a challenge to stand strong in my decision, but I did.

Sometimes, I agreed that if I had stayed, it would have been easier, more convenient, and more comfortable than what I was going through, but when I sat quietly, searched within myself, and stepped into my own awareness, I was reminded of all the reasons why I had moved on, and it became crystal-clear once again who I was now, who I was becoming, and who I was meant to be.

Now, looking back, I see that there were dark days when I sat quietly in the discomfort of my shadows and allowed those restless feelings and limiting beliefs that had been suppressed for so long to come to the surface. Honestly, it scared me and took me by surprise that there was so much darkness, sadness, anger, and unhappiness inside of me. Looking back, feelings of inadequacy, unworthiness, shame about my body, and searching for love outside myself had been keeping me stuck.

I realized that I lived in constant overwhelm and the fear of not being liked, but as time went on and I did the healing, I knew that letting my limiting beliefs, feelings, and emotions come to light would allow me to discover incredible ways to move past them, let them go, and heal my heart.

I discovered that in my darkness there was so much strength, vulnerability, passion, and beauty. The darkness had been there all along to protect me from myself, from others, and from being hurt again. I realized that I no longer needed protection, and by showing myself compassion, forgiveness, and gratitude, I could powerfully move forward in a new direction. So I did!

As each day continued and I had time to be alone and reflect on the past, present, and what I wanted for myself and my daughter in the future, it became easier to face the discomfort, and I was able to face it head-on. With each wound that

41

became a beautiful scar, I confidently and powerfully stepped into the woman I knew I was meant to be.

I began waking up on most days feeling my best physically, spiritually, and energetically. I felt confident and inspired to take action, and that is when I really began attracting and manifesting everything I wanted.

I met the right people at the right time. I was guided to the perfect opportunities that led to additional income, clients, and finally a magnificent partner who aligned with what I wanted and who I had become.

Another wonderful thing happened was the desire to take better care of myself and make myself a priority again. I began putting my needs first. I stopped drinking and overeating as a way to soothe, cope, and forget. I began nourishing my brain and my body with foods that gave me clarity, energy, and helped me to be my best self.

There were days when I would wake up, open my eyes, and think, *Just two years ago I was miserable, and now this is my extraordinary life! YES, I stepped into my courage and my power and I chose this!* Most importantly, I finally felt complete ease, love, and peace within myself. I finally knew all of who I was, and I began attracting all of what I wanted.

I was so inspired by my own journey that I began helping others to create their best health and find love within themselves, and this led to working with women, families, kids, teens, schools, and finally men. I now help men discover the tools they need to feel their very best. I help them learn how to love who they are and powerfully overcome sadness, anger, and unhappiness, and this leads them to attract their perfect partner.

It's so incredible to witness how each one of these men has stepped into their own greatness and discovered their own way to personal healing physically, mentally, and spiritually.

Now, beautiful reader, I want to share the steps I took to get to where I am today, and that have helped so many others. I may not know you, but I know that we all need support, love, and inspiration to get through our challenges. I want to help you discover your own path to healing so you know and truly love all of who you are and attract all of what you want.

It begins with becoming aware of who you are and your situation. It means acknowledging feelings of anger, fear, sadness, and depression. The first step toward being able to move forward is **awareness**.

Secondly, you must develop **clarity** about what you want and who you want to become.

The third step is to replace your old, limiting beliefs with new, **empowering beliefs**. Recognize that those old beliefs were there to protect you, but now they no longer serve you. Take back your power and begin telling yourself a new story. You are a different person now, and you can make empowering choices.

Finally, align yourself with who you are, do the healing, and take **inspired action** in your personal and business life that will bring you joy and attract what you want. Spend time with those you love, take really good care of yourself, and give yourself time to heal, have fun, and connect with people who align with who you are.

In closing, my beautiful friends, awareness, clarity, empowering beliefs, and inspired action helped me get through some of the most difficult times in my life and become the extraordinary woman I am today. You, too, can use these steps to transform your life in the way you want.

I now leave you with these words of love, from my heart to yours:

Ask for what you want.
Love and forgive your shadows.

Believe in yourself.

Take action every time something inspires you.

Take one day, one breath, and one step at a time.

Breathe with ease.

You don't have to have it all figured out right now.

And remember, before you can attract all of what you want, you need to know all of who you are!

Take courage and be brave in your heart.

I love you!

As a Men's Love and Health Coach, **Nancy Benitez** is passionate about helping influential single men stop wasting time, energy, and money on dating women who don't see their value. With her years of experience in personal development, Nancy adds a woman's perspective to help men attract the lasting love they crave and deserve.

www.ManifestWithNancy.com

7. RECEIVING—WHAT'S THAT?

Gina Pero and Dr. David Stella

If you knew that by receiving, you were able to give 100 percent with ease and joy, would you spend more time receiving?

Gina's Story

My name is Gina Pero, and I have learned how to give 100 percent in everything I choose to think, feel, and do. I learned how to give to others—aka, "put others' needs before mine." I learned that in order to receive, I must first give. I embraced the tagline "in giving is receiving" and became a professional giver at an early age. I gave my all, all the way to becoming a Radio City Rockette, where I ended up feeling unfulfilled at the top of the kick-line.

I began to ask myself some questions. *What did I do wrong? What did I miss? What didn't I do? Who was I?* These questions led me to making myself wrong for doing what I had learned. Later I found out that this was a limiting belief. I chose to follow all the guidelines about giving, but I still felt stressed, burned out, and joyless. And then a gift from the Universe flowed into my timeline, and I received it. I moved to Sardinia, Italy, where I began slowly learning how to receive. A new guideline, a new idea, a new way of being, and a new question all led me to feeling fulfilled from the inside out and meeting and receiving my soul partner, Dr. David Stella.

David's Story

My name is Dr. David Stella, and I am a healthcare practitioner and energy facilitator. I like to say that I remove the heavy energy within one's energy field. Many times, we are unaware that these energies are even present. When I choose to facilitate with someone, I first ask these two questions:

- Can I contribute to this person?
- Can they receive from me?

There is a familiar saying from the Bible: "Ask and you shall receive." But what if there are learned patterns from family and friends that put up blocks that make it unable for us to receive? *Hmm . . .*

Within these learned patterns of not receiving, we tend to make ourselves small, wondering why we feel unfulfilled in our relationships at home, with money, and essentially with life.

This is exactly how I felt in 2011, after experiencing a divorce and a declining business.

My journey of asking and receiving began right then in that moment. My focus became learning how to clear and center myself, starting with asking the questions and allowing the answers to be received with discernment. In 2016 this led me to ask the heavenly realm for my soul mate. When I asked the question by being clear and centered first, I knew with 100 percent certainty that I would be able to receive the answer from the Universe with ease, and I learned how to allow the heavenly realm to conspire for me.

As it happened, she walked through my office to see another highly empathic and intuitive practitioner. The practitioner intuitively asked me a question: "Is it light for you and your body to ask Gina out for a coffee?

I became centered in my body through a process I call "clearing," and I then asked these specific questions:

1. Am I a contribution to her?
2. Is she a contribution to me?
3. Will I learn something?
4. Is she fun?
5. Is she expensive?

As I asked the first four questions, I began to receive a light feeling over my chest, which indicates a yes for me and my body. Every person has a unique place in their body in which they can receive a light (or a "yes") feeling. When I asked the question, "Is she expensive?", I received a heavy feeling in my chest, which indicates a "no" for me and my body. Yahoo!

Being in communion with Gina since 2016, we play in this rhythm of what we call light and heavy. This dance with one another is about receiving oneself and receiving each other in choosing and discerning what is light and/or heavy for each of our bodies. We both honor what our bodies can give and receive each day, knowing that the truth of what our bodies require is unique every day.

For example, today we may want to spend time with each other, and tomorrow our bodies may require solitude.

Each day we begin our receiving process by asking our bodies what they need to be living with ease and joy, which we call "light."

The Joy of Receiving

Imagine what your life would feel like if you had a simple process that allowed you to receive exactly what you needed in each moment with ease, joy, and fun.

Imagine knowing how to center and clear your body easily and effortlessly.

Imagine knowing the questions you needed to ask and easily receiving the answers.

Imagine being able to receive 100 percent! Yourself, others, money, career, truth . . .

Well, what have you seen and learned about receiving?

You have simply absorbed learned patterns passed down from past generations.

For example, how often did you see and experience a loving relationship where each person was able to receive compliments, gifts, gestures, food, flowers, money, etc.?

How often did you see and experience the people around you taking time for themselves to center and choosing things that honored their bodies?

How many times did you see your family members use discernment in decisions based on what was light for their bodies, instead of on expectations and projections?

We learn, we copy, we do, and the cycle continues based on old thoughts, feelings, and patterns that have been engrained in our bodies.

What would it feel like to know that these patterns can be easily cleared, allowing you to receive fully?

As a couple, Gina and I experienced many old patterns and many other processes before we both began creating our own process that was easy and quickly effective.

We feel called to show the world a new possibility of what it is like to honor oneself in a soul partnership. We know that in our own journey of healing and clearing ourselves, we also get to heal and clear the planet. We know that every experience we have chosen in this lifetime has led us to learning our own unique process to center ourselves, clear ourselves, ask the questions, and then allow ourselves to receive the answers in divine timing. What we have discovered is that we both have different ways of moving through this process. Every "body" is different, and the way you discover your way of moving through the process is the key ingredient to receiving.

Receiving will be different for each and every one of you. The way you choose to center, clear your energy field, ask the questions, and then allow yourself to receive will be your body's unique way and approach. There is no right, wrong, good, or bad way to receive. Once you learn what ways contribute to your highest and best and nourish your mind, body, and soul, YOU are on your way of receiving. You are on your creative path.

Remember, "ask and you shall receive."

This is a simple process consisting of five steps:

1. Center
2. Clear
3. Ask
4. Allow
5. Receive

As you center yourself in your mind, body, and spirit, you become grounded to the earth and feel connected to the sky. You can then begin your clearing process. After clearing your energy field, your chakras, and whatever else your clearing practice consists of, your body is clearly connected and ready to begin asking the questions.

Once you ask the questions, allowing is the next step, which means accepting the answers in the divine timing as they show up for you now that you are centered and clear. As the answers appear for you, all you need to do next is receive. We like to add the words "Thank you, I receive."

We thank you for receiving our wisdom, insight, and approach to receiving. We thank you for being willing to learn a new process that we know can be beneficial for you as you find your way. And now you can answer the question "Receiving—what's that?"

Gina Pero is an ICF Master Certified Coach who teaches high achieving performers how to easily create a life with ease, joy, and grace. A former Rockette, Gina is the producer of *The Gina Pero Show, The Gina Pero Collection*, and *The Peroettes*.

www.GinaPero.com

Dr. David Stella has owned and operated Stella Chiropractic and Wellness Center since 1998. He teaches people how to easily create freedom in their body, mind, and spirit, focusing on a holistic approach that leads to extraordinary wellness. He travels nationwide and presents with his soul partner, Gina Pero.

www.DrDavidStella.com

8. HEALING THROUGH THE HEART: A GATEWAY TO INTUITIVE BALANCE AND ACTION

Carolyn McGee

My mother had a miscarriage a few months before I was conceived. While she celebrated me, the new pregnancy, she also grieved the loss of the previous child. Is it any wonder that since I was developing while she was grieving, I was born with a heart condition?

I also was born with overdeveloped willpower and determination. This is a characteristic of both my parent's families. I didn't want to be treated differently. I didn't want to accept that there was something wrong with me. My mom was overprotective because she was afraid for me, and I was determined to be treated and act the same as everyone else. This caused me to push myself to excel in everything that I did. I was an honors student. I went to a mainly male college to be an engineer. I was the first person hired by a company in my major. I hiked the Grand Canyon and the Rocky Mountains. I always needed to prove myself and to prove that I was not different.

After many years in high-tech manufacturing, I was exhausted. The pushing energy had taken a toll on my body. My natural heart rate was 40 beats per minute, my adrenals paced my heart, and my body couldn't keep up with my willpower. I had gotten a pacemaker after the birth of my second child, and my body did not know how to deal with the shift in energy. My adrenals were exhausted from me pushing and from them monitoring the rate of my heart for decades. I didn't know how to incorporate the energy shift of the pacemaker and make the connection easy. "Life is difficult" was my mantra.

After passing out from exhaustion in the stockroom at work due to adrenal fatigue, I had to take a partial medical leave to care for myself and reconnect to my own energy. During my leave, I discovered Kundalini Yoga and Reiki. I remembered my connection to myself. I began to understand the way energy flowed in my body and how my emotions factored in. I accepted that life wasn't just logic and willpower. The mind/body connection was part of my awareness.

Shortly after I returned to work full-time work, there was 50 percent reduction in force (including me), and I took the opportunity to follow my heart. I created a pet care business to reconnect with my soul's calling of creating community. As I cared for people's pets, I healed myself and remembered my connection to Source. I dived deep into spiritualism and intuitive connection, and I became a life coach.

But then the energy of extremism came into play again. As I learned more about my spirituality, remembered my intuition, learned to connect with angels, and began communicating with animals, I went to the other extreme again. Instead of being logical and using willpower as I did in the first part of my life, I sometimes forgot that I lived in a body; I lived in my head, trusting Spirit to take care of me. "The Universe has my back" became my mantra to the point where I would sometimes forget to pay my bills, reply to emails, act on intuitive downloads, or care for my body.

In one of my classes, I learned how to use a pendulum, and I realized that this extreme one way or the other energy that I was living was like the energy of a pendulum that was undecided. The big swing back and forth and not settling on an answer so that action or a decision could be taken was paralyzing. I was in constant movement, but I was not moving forward to be of service to those who needed me. This understanding helped me to bring those shifts back into balance and center.

I realized that our hearts are the center of our energy fields. I could see that logically from the chakra map with the heart, the fourth chakra, being right in the middle of the seven embodied chakras. What I didn't realize at the time is that it is also the energetic center of heaven and earth: inspiration and action; divine feminine and divine masculine.

Once again, I was experiencing an imbalance between logical and spiritual energy: the energy of inspiration and action. As I continued to grow personally and work deeper with my coaching clients, I realized that there is often a disconnect in the energy between the lower three chakras that are connected to earth energy and being grounded in our physical body to act and the upper three chakras that are connected to spirituality and vision.

My clients seemed to be so focused on connecting to spirit, speaking their truth, and receiving intuitive connection that they forgot to integrate that divine energy into their physical bodies. The guidance just lived in their upper chakras, and they didn't act on the wisdom.

It came to me that if we can't wash that energy up and down our bodies through our physical hearts, then we have the same kind of divide that I had in the past with my logical mind and my spiritual mind. The more work I did with clients (as well as with myself), the more frustrated I got, but I couldn't seem to break through that energetic barrier of the heart block.

During one of my personal meditations, I remembered the details of my congenital heart condition, and I discovered why it was so profoundly important for me on this journey. The type of heart condition I have is called a "complete heart block." This means that the natural pacemaker that should set the rhythm for my heart does not pick up the signal that is sent out. There is a complete block of the signal from source to action.

Imagine that there is a radar signal being sent out; in a normal heart it knows to slow your heart rate down when you rest, and it knows to increase your heart rate because you're frightened or excited and you need a little bit more blood flow through your body. In my case, it was as if there was a steel plate between the two sides of my heart, and even though both the sending part and the receiving part were working perfectly, they couldn't talk to each other. I was disconnected.

As I clearly saw this, I realized that my heart chakra was also blocking the divine feminine and the divine masculine from connecting in my physical and energetic body. That inspirational source information was not connecting to the grounded "take action" part of me.

I saw the same thing in my clients. It was hard for them to take action on the brilliant divine inspiration they received, as it didn't flow through their hearts. Instead they would act from a place of fear, that energy that lives in our body when we're not spiritually connected in the truth.

Once I recognized the truth of this, I felt my heart burst open and expand just like the Grinch when "his small heart grew three sizes that day." I felt all those past challenges line up into an awareness of the gift of the power of trusting and feeling energy in our hearts. The knowledge that our hearts are the gateway to connection and power solidified for me.

I knew that our hearts are our most intuitive muscle and always know the truth. Our hearts are the gatekeeper of energy between source and action. Our hearts are the path to clarity, peace, and manifestation.

Now I can connect the divine masculine inspirational intuitive energy and divine feminine grounded action-taking energy and wash it through my Sacred Heart. By doing this, I know the truth of what my next right step is, trusting myself to take empowered action—and I can help my clients to do the same thing. We can all open to that full body flow of energy that is so critical for us to live a full and connected life.

Intuitive Strategist and Coach **Carolyn McGee** specializes in Amplifying YOUR Intuitive Superpower to understand, trust, and follow your soul's path to live a joyful, abundant, and purposeful life. She helps you remember your connection to your intuition to enhance receiving messages, trust your guidance 24/7, and take empowered action.

www.CarolynMcGee.com

9. CAN YOU RELATE?

RaShawn-Renée

The World Health Organization refers to it as among the greatest atrocities of human rights. Yet many of us don't see or know the warning signs because we haven't examined our pathology in order to understand our susceptibility. The statistics clearly show that this is a global epidemic. The facts are inescapable, affecting one out of three women globally and 69 percent of the women in the United States. The statistics for men are one out of ten globally and 52 percent in the United States. This atrocity absolutely affects the whole of humanity.

The atrocity that I'm writing about is physical and sexual violence in relationships; our society calls it domestic abuse, which usually stems from psychological abuse. Many of us are willing to endure that which we once perceived as unimaginable for a long while before deciding to make the courageous choice to leave. Still others for many reasons make the choice to stay and live a life of marginal existence.

Have you courageously chosen your path, or do you just accept your unexamined conditioning?

I lived through an experience of abuse that could have devastated me for the rest of my life. However, the experience forced me to grow, learn more about me, discover more about life, and reveal my story, which gave me the gift of releasing shame and unexamined conditioning. I wrote a book that further expanded my understanding and awareness. From the point of Awareness came a mission, and this is why I know that the whole of my life and your life are ALL NECESSARY for our evolution.

I made the courageous choice to leave an abusive relationship, and if I had not left, I would have never spoken at the University of Quito in Ecuador. I would never have received a thunderous standing ovation in London after speaking on International Women's Day to a packed ballroom. I would never have seen the lives of women and men change from the impact of what I teach them. I would never have built an organization that teaches how to gain wholeness-of-self and honors life. I would never have experienced the emotional, psychological, and spiritual growth within our family. I would never have written *44 Hours & 21 Minutes: A Woman's Truth and Power*, a book that up-levels the thinking of each reader and on its merits has been compared to Michelle Obama's bestselling book *Becoming*. I would have never gotten to see and know the Real Me.

I wonder: Is this your time to make a courageous choice?

I thought I had it all together, and the only thing that seemed to be missing according to everyone and everything in my sphere (family, friends, colleagues, magazines, television, etc.) was my Prince Charming. The ideology projected upon me was that having a man by my side would make me significant, because being single made me insignificant. My business would increase just by others knowing that I was in a committed relationship. So, when I met the guy that was supposed to fulfill my fantasy, I was devasted when the fairy tale abruptly ended. From there, I proceeded into a seemingly unfathomable nightmare.

In the beginning, what I secretly believed and what others told me about being in a relationship was happening. My business went from great to astonishingly great, and I enjoyed my work and social life more. Colleagues who were married invited us to dinner parties. It was picture-perfect—being in a relationship made life better. The fairy tale looked and felt really good for a while . . . and then he had an affair. The relationship ended, and deep down inside of me, I felt discarded and broken. I tried to convince myself that I was fine. I couldn't admit to myself or anyone else that I was unequipped to handle what I was experiencing. So I pretended to be strong, unscathed by betrayal, resilient, smart, and ready to move forward with my life.

I moved forward by moving away from my family and everything familiar to me. I accepted an invitation to visit a man, who in our first conversation communicated his reverence for women and his disdain for people who were unfaithful in their relationships. That was all I needed to hear to choose him.

Within an hour of our first date, though, I knew he wasn't for me. And instead of not having a second date, I made us a couple. From the beginning, I began looking the other way, pretending I wasn't seeing what I saw. By the second date, I was justifying his behavior and making excuses for his demeaning language. On many occasions he said, "I'd rather be feared than loved." He would also say: "I love you, and you can never leave me." I thought I could change him, fix him, make him a better person. I convinced myself that he was a good man because he loathed infidelity. I said yes to a man because being in a relationship made me significant; it was proof that I was valuable. I said yes to that relationship because I didn't know my Real Truth and how to live with Power.

Do you know your Real Truth and how to live with Power?

We moved into a beautiful house he purchased for us, and in the midst of decorating it, I knew I had to leave. I had left him before and let him convince me to come back with the guarantee things would be different. Things were different for a while, and then they got worse than before. He cursed me, threw things, threatened me, and did other things to show his strength and his desire to rule over my body and life. I knew that if I didn't leave him, he would eventually really hurt me, or even kill me.

I attempted several times to have a conversation with him about ending the relationship, yet after each conversation, he would do something very thoughtful, be especially kind, and say: "I love you; no one is going to love you the way I love you. You can't leave me—I won't allow it!"

Finally, I stopped trying to have amicable conversations about leaving him and made up my mind: it was time to leave. I escaped from the house and ended the relationship. My escape revealed that he was willing to do anything to make me return to him. In his mind, I was going to be his fiancée and then his wife; I was going to live in that house, do what he wanted, and never leave him. He was determined to get me back, and I was courageously committed to never return to him. When I repeatedly refused to return to him on my own accord, he and his best friend did something that was unthinkable.

He had given me access to all his credit cards and bank accounts for my personal use and to help manage the accounts. So, I was shocked in a state of disbelief when I was arrested and charged with identity theft and credit card fraud. Hours after being taken into custody, I was wearing an orange jumpsuit and being escorted through a corridor with such a foul smell, it triggered a gag response. I would have vomited if I wasn't so occupied by taking in visually what was in front of me. I saw a toilet affixed to the wall with a basin next to it. Two steps away from the basin were bunk beds, and on the bottom bunk there was a woman who scared me, and yet I knew she wouldn't harm me. There was a small padded cover on the top bunk (similar to a mattress) . . . I was standing in front of a jail cell.

I stepped into the cell carrying the pillowcase (the official welcome to jail package given to me when I put on the jumpsuit) containing a sheet, toothpaste, toothbrush, and an apple. The woman in the cell stood up as I entered, looked me up and down, turned around, and began reaching for something at the end of her bunk. When she turned around, she had a Bible in her hand and said, "This is for you, and can I have your apple?" I gave her the apple, and she showed me how to get to the top bunk. I climbed up, made a pillow by using the items in the pillowcase, and added the Bible. That night in the jail cell provided moments that would ultimately define themselves as the impetus for me to learn my Real Truth and choose to live with Power. Those moments set the stage for self-love, compassion, and the desire for greater understanding of myself, life, and how I got there. It also began my quest to find out why so many people live in quiet desperation.

Life gets better when you choose YOU!

Morning came, the cell doors opened, and with tears streaming down my face, I quickly jumped down from the top bunk with a steadiness of self I hadn't experienced until that moment. As my feet hit the floor, I knew I was different.

Over time I have awakened to living my Real Truth and Power by releasing the familial and societal conditioning that doesn't contribute to a life of inner peace, fulfillment, joy, and the eradication of shame and feelings of insignificance. Each day is a Dream Come True because I get to experience the Real Me—the Me with Whole-Self-Acceptance. The Me that engages all of life for learning and teaches others to do the same.

We can create the world we want to live in by revealing the person we want to be. You are Magnificent. I am Magnificent, and we can live a magnificent life when we know our Real Truth and Power.

RaShawn-Renée is a woman committed to You—committed to You experiencing an outstanding life. Your life propels forward, ascends higher, expands wider, and spirals to its depth, and when you engage with her teachings, every area of your life will be enhanced. Author, speaker, and You'ist™ are among the distinctions for this woman of valor.

www.RealTruthIntl.com

10. PAIN, BREATH, AND THE BUTTERFLY EFFECT

Jana Danielson

You might be wondering: What do pain, breath, and the Butterfly Effect have in common? That is exactly what I am going to tell you. These three phenomena are the defining factors of my highest of highs and my lowest of lows. These three phenomena created chaos in my life, they forced me to look differently at who I was, they challenged me to think differently about the life I wanted to live, and they helped me to realize exactly what I was put here on this Earth to do. Through the story of pain, breath, and the Butterfly Effect, I hope I can offer you moments of thoughtful reflection and intentional analysis into your life so you can really connect with who you are and who you are meant to be.

Pain

I am the firstborn of three kids. Growing up in the heart of the Canadian Prairies provided us with wide open spaces to play, a huge garden to grow our own vegetables, and friends whom we met in kindergarten and graduated high school with. In my case, a bonus was finding my future husband in this small community of five hundred amazing people. Entrepreneurial DNA ran thick in our family, and ideas were encouraged, teamwork was required, and doing whatever was needed to get the job done was a given. There is no better upbringing I could have hoped for.

My life was not all roses, though. During high school I began to experience pain. This pain came and went, such as during times when I was getting ready to take an exam, preparing my farewell speech for my high school graduation, or waiting for my boyfriend to call me when he was late. This pain was like a ball of burning fire spinning in my stomach. It became a regular part of my life, and my family just chalked it up to me being a nervous high achiever. The pain got so bad during my university days that I named it "My Edge." I needed to give it a personality so I could acknowledge it and trick my brain into thinking that I would ace the test or get the job if "My Edge" was along for the ride. As long as I had "My Edge" with me, I was ready for whatever came at me.

In my early twenties, I visited doctor after doctor, specialist after specialist. Over a nine-month period, not one of those professionals could help me; all the tests they gave me turned up no diagnosis. "My Edge" did not want a new name. With each subsequent visit, there were no answers, but there was more medication. I was on a grocery list of meds, with some meds only prescribed to deal with the side effects of other meds. At the time, I was newly engaged and had my first job after completing my business degree. I knew I wanted to be a mom one day, but I had no idea how I could have a successful marriage, career, or life if I had to live this way for the rest of my life. On one of my last visits, the doctor told me that there was nothing more that could be done for me—that this pain most likely was all in my head and that I was seeking attention. It was the lowest of lows. Now what?

Breath

Standing in line at the grocery store one day in the fall of 1999, I saw Madonna on the cover of *Shape* magazine. The word *Pilates* was diagonally typeset across her picture. I had no idea what that was, but as a huge fan of the Material Girl, if she was doing something new, I wanted to try it.

I discovered that there was a twice-a-week Pilates class not far from my house, and I immediately called to sign up. My husband, Jason, went with me to the gym on the first day of class, but headed to the weight room—he thought that Pilates was just for women.

I walked in wearing the new leggings I bought for this momentous occasion and gripping my new Pilates mat. There were about a dozen other people, a mix of men and women (note to self: Jason was coming with me next time), but all older than me. My competitive spirit kicked in, and I anticipated being the best Pilates student in that class. Wrong, wrong, wrong. When the instructor started to cue us through the basics of the Pilates breath, which is diaphragmatic breathing, I had nothing, zero, nada. My belly would not smoothly rise on the inhale and melt on the exhale. I felt tension throughout my entire body, as if I was protecting myself from myself! Normally an experience like this would have me running for the hills. But something different happened to me that night. My lack of connection between my brain and my body intrigued me. What was going on (or in my case what was NOT going on) in my body that would not allow me to breathe properly? Isn't breathing something that is just supposed to happen without really having to think about it?

I played all kinds of sports as a kid, taught aerobics through university to help pay for tuition, did bootcamps, and ran marathons, yet I could not get my main respiratory muscle, my diaphragm, to do its job. My diaphragm was supposed to be my breathing muscle; it was supposed to fill my trillions of cells with the oxygen they needed to flourish. I was determined to find it.

Week after week I went to my mat class. I hung on my instructor's every word, and I practiced on the days that I was not in class. After six weeks I started to notice something BIG. Before Pilates, if I forgot to take my meds at the precise time each day, "My Edge" would remind me and throw me into a whirlwind of pain. Six weeks into my Pilates life, I noticed that it was 1:00 p.m. and I should have taken my meds at noon. I was an hour late, and my pain was not bad. Eight weeks into my Pilates life, things continued to improve. I had not told anyone about this yet as I did not want to jinx whatever was going on with me. "My Edge" still visited in those days, but it was a much more watered-down version. Twelve weeks into my Pilates life, I noticed other changes in my body. My blood sugar did not drop as drastically during the day and those "hangry" moments disappeared. I was sleeping better, eating better, hydrating my body better, and my physique started to change. This form of exercise didn't cause my joints to strain, and I did not have to sweat profusely or spend hours a week at the gym—and it was changing my body in ways no other exercise had. I was hooked.

I literally found my breath through Pilates. This simple act of finding my breath changed my life.

The Butterfly Effect

The Butterfly Effect is a part of Chaos Theory that states that a small, localized change in a complex system can have large effects elsewhere. In essence, a butterfly flapping its wings at the precise space and time in North America can cause a hurricane across the world. To me, the Butterfly Effect means that even the smallest things can have a huge impact on your life and that in the midst or aftermath of chaos, beauty can emerge.

As I reflect on my journey, I realize that it was through my pain that I lost my breath. I went to business school, completed both my undergraduate and graduate degrees, and was achieving my corporate ladder aspirations. "My Edge" silenced me in a way; it was like I was just going through the motions. Now, don't get me wrong—I had an amazing husband, a good job, and I was happy, but there came a point where that was not enough. I needed something that gave me passion and purpose; I wanted to make a difference.

Through my pain I lost my voice, because you can't have a voice if you do not have breath. Through finding my breath, I found my voice. Through finding my voice, I found my passion, and through finding my passion, I found my purpose.

I became certified as a Pilates instructor in 2008 and started teaching four classes a week out of our home to my friends and family. By 2010 I was teaching sixteen classes a week and scheduling twenty hours of private sessions a week. Jason convinced me that the hobby I was so passionate about was turning into a business that I also could be passionate about.

In September 2010, we opened Lead Pilates, our first 2,200-square-foot Pilates studio. In 2015 Lead Pilates expanded into our current 9,000-square-foot facility, and we added Lead Integrated Health Therapies to the mix. My team of more than fifty amazing individuals gets to educate, inspire, and move the clients and patients who choose to walk through our doors every day to become better versions of themselves.

In the fall of 2019, I launched the Metta District, which is my online Pilates studio, and now I can impact lives all over the world! My latest passion project was launched in April 2020 in the middle of the pandemic: my patented pelvic floor fitness tools, the Cooch Ball (for women) and the Gooch Ball (for men), were born. I am impacting lives today because I believed there was a better way to heal the body. I am impacting lives because I connected with my soul purpose. I am confident that, no matter what your situation is, you can find your soul purpose too!

Jana Danielson is a wife, mom of three teenage sons, and a champion for health and wellness. Her own health issues were the catalyst for a career shift over twelve years ago from the world of corporate consulting to that of wellness entrepreneur. A believer in wellness from the inside out, Jana is eager to share her philosophy, hints and tips with you!

www.mettadistrict.com

11. CELEBRATE YOU FIRST

Renée Porteous

It was May 27, 2016, the last day of kindergarten for my twins, Eden and Xen, and a day that changed all of our lives forever.

Flashback to April when I had found a lump in my right breast, something I had not noticed before. I chalked it up to "that time of the month" and went about my business, but when some time had passed and the lump had not, I knew it required further investigation.

Back to May 27th. We picked the kids up from school, and we were ready to celebrate our kids' kindergarten graduation—but not before a quick stop at the imaging center where I could pick up the results from my breast biopsy that I was sure would report some benign condition.

I ran into the imaging center, returned back to the car with the biopsy report in hand, ready to read the results. The next words out of my mouth began the moment that changed who I am forever. "I have breast cancer, Mark."

My husband, thinking I was joking, said, "That's not funny. You are joking! You are joking, right?"

Tears began to stream down my face as I began my spiral down the rabbit hole. *Oh my god, the kids just turned six; they just had their last day of kindergarten today, and I don't know how serious this cancer is. Am I going to die? Am I going to see my kids grow up? I am too young. Why me?*

Although it was still a while before I knew the seriousness of my breast cancer and what lay ahead for me in my near future, I did make drastic changes in my life immediately. You see, I had been working really hard. Between volunteering at school, helping my husband run his business, having clients of my own, and trying to be Wonder Woman, I was failing.

I had stopped working out regularly because I thought I had too much to do and not enough time to do it. I had stopped eating well because there was never time to stop and make myself something healthy. All of this was making me angry and resentful. I was full of negative emotions along with the exhaustion from working all hours of the day and night.

All of that stopped the day I found out I had cancer.

It was time for me to focus on myself. I had been doing a fantastic job of taking care of everyone else, but I had been severely neglecting my own needs.

My husband, Mark, always uses the oxygen mask analogy. If you have ever flown, you know the speech. The flight attendant will announce, "In the event of a decompression, an oxygen mask will automatically appear in front of you. To start the flow of oxygen, pull the mask toward you. Place it firmly over your nose and mouth, secure the elastic band behind your head, and breathe normally. . . . If you are traveling with a child or someone who requires assistance, secure your mask first and then assist the other person."

I had to start putting on my own oxygen mask, that day and every day thereafter. I needed to take care of myself. I needed to not just survive but thrive so I could watch my children grow into the amazing people they were becoming. I would be no good to anyone if I didn't take care of myself first!

So what did putting on the oxygen mask look like for me? Well, the first thing I had to do was learn to say "no." I am notorious for overcommitting myself to help others out with projects. My normal "yes" turned to "No, I am sorry, but I am not available" or "Let me get back to you."

I also had to start setting boundaries. I began setting times and days that I was available for work and volunteer projects. I didn't need to make myself available 24/7.

The woman who never had enough time to even grab a healthy snack now spent twenty minutes a day juicing (sometimes multiple times a day). I also began to take time to meditate and get fresh air and exercise daily. I began practicing what my husband called extreme self-care.

During my five months of chemotherapy, that extreme self-care served me well. Other than all of my hair falling out, which was unavoidable due to the type of chemo I was receiving, I had no side effects from treatment. Every visit, I received confirmation from the doctors and nurses on staff to keep doing whatever I was doing because it was clearly working.

As a result of all of my new self-care practices, the concept of Celebrate You First was conceived during my chemotherapy treatment. I had just received my second dose of "the red devil" and was pumped full of steroids and anti-nausea medicine. As I thought about what I wanted to create with Celebrate You First, I envisioned a grand event that would celebrate women, self-care, and self-love—with hundreds of women coming together to celebrate themselves!

Until I could create this spectacular event, I decided I would blog, so I bought the URL CelebrateYouFirst.com and began my blogging journey. My goal was to focus on self-care, especially nutrition and wellness, as that is my background.

Somewhere along the way, I began to feel like every post revolved around my journey with cancer. During cancer treatment, I didn't even share with most people that I had cancer, so why would I want to constantly rehash it in a blog?

When I started sporting a wig during treatment, many people just thought I was having fun with a new hairstyle. No one questioned it because on the outside I seemed to be pretty healthy, just really thin with some funky eyelash and eyebrow issues. I was still running outdoors, I continued to work, I still helped out at school regularly as a room parent, and I volunteered at any event I could. Yes, there were days I felt like crap, but for the most part, no one knew that I was fighting cancer unless I had shared my story with them.

By not sharing my story, I had a layer of protection—a layer of protection for my children and myself. I didn't want people treating my kids differently, especially at school. When I did finally stop wearing my wig and my hair was really short, a girl in my daughter's class began taunting my daughter. "Ha, ha, ha, your mommy has no hair." My daughter came home crying. How can first graders be so cruel? This just confirmed that the layer of protection I had created served its purpose . . . until it didn't.

The short hair brought questions, and I finally started sharing. People I had told in confidence also started sharing, and that was that. It didn't become a big thing. I didn't allow it to. I didn't want cancer to define me. I didn't want my identity to revolve around the fact that I had cancer. But now with my blog, Celebrate You First, here I was, rehashing my experience with cancer in every post that I wrote.

You see, I think as humans we often can get stuck in our story, and although breast cancer is definitely part of my story, it doesn't define me, and it is in no way my whole story. I happily took the experience and learned from it, but I just didn't want to talk about cancer, so I stopped writing my Celebrate You First blog and moved on. On to the next chapter of my life!

Besides learning to make myself a priority, if cancer taught me anything, it is to live in each moment.

I am living my life to the fullest, celebrating what matters most, and writing the next chapter of my life's story. I did discover that I enjoy blogging, so now I'm sharing my passion on my Florida Fun Family blog, which is all about my family's adventures and celebrating the moments that matter most, the moments of being together as a family.

Practicing extreme self-care allows me to follow my passion while continuing to support high-level transformational leaders with systems and structures to give them more time and freedom to do what they love.

There are still days when I have to remind myself to put on my oxygen mask first, because I am by nature a nurturer and want to take care of everyone. Yes, it felt selfish at times in the beginning to really take care of myself and put myself first, and occasionally it still does, but I just remind myself that I am no good to anyone if I don't take care of me too. So I will continue to **Celebrate Me First**!

Renée Porteous could be described as a wife, mother, and breast cancer survivor, but none of those titles could tell the complete story of who she is. Renee is a woman who wears many hats, spending her days helping her husband with his business, supporting transformational leaders, and volunteering her time to her children's school.

www.ReneePorteous.com

Part Two

CONNECTING TO YOUR SOUL OFFER

Do you believe you're here for a reason?

What does "Life Purpose" mean to YOU?

The True Purpose Institute teaches four aspects of purpose: Your Essence, Your Blessing, Your Message, and Your Mission. Defining these aspects of your purpose communicates who you are, who you help, how you help them, AND your BIG why.

Eckhart Tolle, one of the most sought-after spiritual teachers of our time, teaches two universal types of purpose:

1. Inner Purpose = Being (achieved through personal development)
2. Outer Purpose = Doing (achieved through service to others)

When your Being and Doing are aligned, you are "On Purpose."

This is often reflected as "Authenticity—being real and transparent."

How does your Purpose relate to Health, Wealth, and Love?

You can Monetize Your Message by building a business in alignment with your Values, Vision, and Mission.

Being "On Purpose" creates flow, synchronicity, and opportunities to grow your business while evolving personally.

When you are living in alignment with your Soul Purpose, you open yourself to attract amazing people who are also living in alignment. Being On-Purpose naturally attracts more Love into your life.

The stories in Part Two will help provide you with a greater clarity about your unique Soul Purpose.

12. FOLLOWING THE GOLDEN THREAD

Holly Woods, PhD

More people than ever imagine that purpose is an indicator of living a successful life—more than wealth, a prestigious career, or positions of notoriety—and for good reason. Purpose affects personal income and wealth, the financial performance of a business, employee engagement, leadership, job satisfaction, longevity, acute and chronic health conditions, mental health and well-being, emotional regulation, memory and cognition, and relationships. Knowing your purpose—and living it—positively affects every facet of your life.

Yet most people aren't ready, able, or willing to do what is required to accomplish these significant outcomes, even though they crave lives of greater contribution, fulfillment, and satisfaction.

No one is born knowing their purpose; we must embark on a search to find our purpose. This search can be daunting, stressful, and an isolating endeavor, especially without guidance. Victor Frankl, who wrote *Man's Search for Meaning* back in 1946, observed that the search process itself often leads to inner tension, frustration, and distress.

This "purpose anxiety," however, is well worth the discomfort when you consider the abundance of positive life outcomes associated with living a purposeful life.

The search for purpose is key to discovering your true identity and the path to finding your way home to yourself.

Many steps in your lifetime may appear to take you in the *wrong* direction. From this, you learn that each circumstance or tragedy offers you two gifts: first, a glimpse into the "shadow" side of your identity, and second, the "gift" of recalibrating your focus so you can be more intentional and directed toward your purpose.

Coming to grips with "finding yourself," making your greatest contribution, despite and because of your shadows and struggles, is what allows you to "come home" to yourself and begin living your purpose. It infuses every cell of your being with the dynamic energy of inspiration, and ultimately synchronicity.

How Purpose Runs through Your Life

Your purpose is a Golden Thread that is the "through-line" in your life's tapestry. As Michael Meade described it: "The soul is threaded through with a plotline from the beginning that aims at a destiny that might be possible to find before the end."

The Golden Thread was there at birth, and possibly in many other lives. It represents the longing and expression of your unique Soul Purpose. In addition, **you are the only one with this unique Golden Thread of Purpose. There is no other "thread" like yours.**

Living On Purpose is about becoming more of who you are, and less of who you are not.

I've arrived at three hypotheses about purpose that will help you claim your own.

Hypothesis One: Purpose Is Our GPS

We're always on purpose. Our soul is always pulling us in the direction of a fuller expression of our authentic nature. We just don't recognize it, or we can't see it.

In any lifetime, you can see an unlimited number of "expressions" of purpose. These expressions are more than just a career, job, or project, and they are only limited by your availability to hear the "calling" to live into your next expression. As you hear the call, you garner the capabilities or resources to move into that expression with ease.

If this hypothesis is true, purpose feels like a "pull" or a longing that generates reactions such as passion, creativity, love, or excitement, and this pull helps you decide whether an invitation or a decision is in alignment with your true nature. It also may show up as fear, trepidation, anxiety, or shadow force, if you're fighting against your wounding to be more of yourself.

Hypothesis Two: Purpose Is Hidden by Your Wounding

Childhood wounding causes you to become someone other than yourself. When your childhood is healthy enough, you know yourself by the things that delight you. You might love animals or nature, are inspired by music or art, or build things and take them apart. While the objects you "like" are usually not your purpose, the manner in which you explore the content and how or why it delights you is an indicator of your true inspiration.

You may have experienced an optimal "self-knowing" in childhood that helped you identify with the natural expressions of purpose. If so, you came to know yourself more clearly and could hear the callings to explore.

But what if instead of this optimal self-awareness, you weren't given the attention, resources, or encouragement to pursue your own interests? Your identity then would have been shaped around what others wanted you to be, thus creating an inconsistent or repressed version of who you really are.

When a child doesn't develop an adequate level of self-awareness or self-identity, their authentic nature and deepest soul desires are suppressed. This suppression leads to an overt expression of the childhood wound, rather than the authentic gifts of purpose.

As childhood wounding plays out over our lifespan, it will look different at each stage of life and hide our purposeful identity until we resolve the "self-knowing" wound. This process is the substance of the "shadowed" part of personality. Uncovering who we really are often becomes too painful after childhood because we've stuffed it down so far.

As we resolve our childhood (or later) wounding, our purpose becomes more evident, and we become more fully expressed and able to contribute our unique, one-of-a-kind genius.

If this hypothesis is true, our life is the "school" that trains us to overcome the challenges of our childhood and live meaningful lives. It is the transformational fodder for our human development. We can only evolve into more aware humans and grow purposefully if we can see ourselves and our "circumstances" in a new light.

But when we're in the midst of a serious trauma, we see ourselves as victims, which further calcifies our identity that shaped around our childhood wounds. In fact, the wounding is the "mirror" image (or flip side) of the purposeful gift itself. What we didn't accomplish in childhood or later is played out through our "inner children," which are repressed sub-psychic parts that fracture during our childhood and ultimately express in rebellious or diminished ways. These "parts" are often hidden to the individual—and thus, the "shadow"—but seen quite markedly as part of the egoic personality by everyone around us. Resolution of these shadow wounds must be focused on the stage of development in which the wound was formed so that the integration of the fractured part can be accomplished fully.

Hypothesis Three: Expression of Purpose Varies by Developmental Stage

Purpose remains "hidden" unless you can see it through the filters of your stage of life. During each phase of life, the developmental tasks needed to "ripen" into your next stage require you to expand your perspective or "worldview." As you develop into each next stage of life, you gain the capacity to "see" contexts more broadly—and to heal your wounding—giving you the chance to see your purpose even more clearly.

Thus, the "thread" of your purpose, which would be more readily seen if not for the wounding that hides it from you, is also more apparent if you are looking for the most likely expression in any given developmental phase.

If this hypothesis is true, the threads of purpose show up in simple form at each developmental stage, building in complexity as you become more nuanced and context-aware over your lifespan. Early expressions of purpose will look like self-exploration, relationship development, and development of principles and values. Later expressions of purpose are more nuanced and expressed in the world through individual or collective action.

In each tier of your lifespan, the expression of purpose shifts from a "being" stage to a "becoming" stage. This process is a constantly iterative cycle that includes and integrates earlier tasks of development into each subsequent stage.

Your soul "longs" to express itself as true authentic nature and goes to great effort to ensure that you complete your developmental tasks by offering you circumstances that "trigger" you to confront the wounding that keeps your purpose hidden. These "triggers" are merely mirrors of your own shadow. They are opportunities to do the deep work to liberate you from the constrained identity that buries your purpose.

Four Guiding Principles to Find Your Purpose and Do What Matters Most

How would you live your life if nothing stood in the way of your ultimate fulfillment and your grandest gesture? Rather than searching for money, fame, or prestige, what would you do if you knew you couldn't fail?

Guiding Principle One: Awareness

Awareness—of yourself, the community of humans, and the "more-than-human world" around you—is by far the most significant, pressing, and compelling precept of our time. If we cannot truly know ourselves and each other, we cannot solve this mess.

Guiding Principle Two: Alignment

Alignment consists of three elements. First, you need clarity about who you are, which includes the essence of your purpose. This quality allows you to make your greatest purposeful contribution and have your biggest impact.

Second, gaining confidence is foundational for who you really are, as opposed to living from who you are not. Over time, you'll learn to witness the patterns that keep you shackled to the status quo (e.g., limiting beliefs, fears, self-judgment, criticism, distractions, bad habits, fractured ego parts, and misguided intentions) and enable you to live a life of possibility.

Third, you'll learn specifically about your contribution, that which you are meant to do, your primary driver or burning desire. You'll create a purpose statement and learn how to live "as if" you are on purpose and in a state of flow, which is a direct expression of being on purpose.

Guiding Principle Three: Agility

Agility requires physical grace and speed, mental processing skills that are faster than your typical daily routines, and the "nimble" or flexible state that allows you to respond to numerous swiftly moving pieces. This agility also allows you to respond uniquely to shifts occurring in your world, the kind that are typical when your life and work evolve quickly. As you engage in purposeful pursuits, the need to adapt your actions and identity to the incoming feedback is best approached through an agile and responsive action and mindset.

Guiding Principle Four: Amplify

Once the first three steps to uncover and live into your purpose have created a solid foundation of increased focus, meaning, joy, abundance, and greater contribution, your purpose begins to amplify almost of its own accord through a series of small, then growing, synchronistic events. These occurrences may seem like magic at first, as people appear out of nowhere to contribute solutions to your everyday dilemmas, or to connect you with someone who has an important piece to your puzzle. Time and space almost seem nonexistent when you get to this stage. As these forms of synchronicity begin to happen, the time has definitely come to claim your purpose, because you've found your current expression as magically as one can find it.

In conclusion, the key to living on purpose is to look squarely in the face of your greatest sorrows and greatest joys, find the connection between them over time, and understand that they are flip sides of the same coin. Joy is the expression of light; sorrow is the expression of the dark. Neither are right or wrong, and both illuminate who you really are.

Holly Woods, PhD, guides you to discover and activate your soul purpose to gain capacity and mindset to attain unreasonable goals and align your life and work around what matters most. She is a speaker and the bestselling author of *The Golden Thread: Where to Find Purpose in the Stages of Your Life*.

www.EmergenceInstitute.net

13. SACRED CONTRACTS DECODED—THE ROADMAP TO YOUR TRUE HOME

Ollga Belova

Celestial Mother glanced at her charts—perfect alignment! It was time to gather those who had come of age to embark on the epic journey into the faraway lands to claim their destiny.

She invited them into the Great Hall for the final instructions. Grown as they were, they still behaved like excited teenagers at a graduation—full of effervescent obliviousness.

Celestial Mother, unfazed by their giddiness, proceeded to give them instructions.

"My dear children," she said, "you've come a long way in your studies, and now it's time for you to step into your next great task that we have extensively discussed and that you have agreed to.

"These agreements are recorded in our Sacred Language, which makes them irrevocable. They must be activated immediately, and to do that, each one of you will embark on a journey to one of four lands. Each land has ten castles, guarded by ten dragons. Each castle is surrounded by a lush garden.

"Your task is to tame the dragon, as the dragon's power opens the door to the castle and grants you the rightful ownership of the castle as your homestead; otherwise you will neither enter the castle, nor will you be able to leave its grounds.

"You must take care of the garden, for its fruit will make your life in the castle abundant and prosperous; otherwise you will always be lacking and suffering.

"Obey the laws of your land; otherwise your life will be full of conflict and struggle."

The task was both simple and seemingly impossible—how would they know where to find those lands? And how would they know how to tame the dragons? And gardening? They had never studied that.

Celestial Mother knew better than to give them more instructions—they had to discover everything on their own, and all that was needed was already recorded in their Sacred Contracts. She also knew that the Sacred Contracts had to be stored in such a way that they would never be lost. When she kissed each of her children goodbye, her celestial energy imprinted the contract into their hands.

Their journeys were long and difficult, and by the time they had reached their destinations, many had forgotten how to read the Sacred Language and forgot their contracts. Some got distracted by shiny things, for faraway lands were full of shiny things.

Those who remembered or figured out their contract, found and tamed their dragons and got to enjoy a blissful life in their castles. Those who never did camped at the gates—near the castle but never inside, yet unable to leave. Have you seen their tents? What if you are in one of them?

—The Second Story Ever Told

This story is a metaphor for our soul journey through the human experience on this planet to provide us with guidance on how to navigate toward a life of meaning and prosperity. Like any mythic story, The Second Story is rich in symbolism that taps into fundamental aspects of each of us as human beings.

When we come into this world in the physical human form, we are composed of three major parts. One, the most obvious, is our physical structure ordered by our DNA code gifted to us by our ancestors. Second, ever-expanding, deeply stored, and often below the level of conscious memories, are the past life experiences that influence tastes, preferences, and talents. Third, the enduring, permanent, and non-destructible core is the soul.

The hero's journey is our quest to find our true home—the energetic place where the soul can feel its connection to the source in this lifetime, inside our Castle. Both Castles and Dragons are archetypal patterns that are familiar to human experience—Success/Failure, Power/Victimhood, Control/Surrender, to name a few. The Castles signify the high-end expression of an archetype, while the Dragons are the low-end expressions.

Life in the Castle is the reward for undertaking the journey and taming the Dragon—the low end of the energetic spectrum and thus far unfamiliar to one's soul experience. Essentially, we come into this life not for the life in the Castle; rather, we are here to tame the Dragon.

The Garden with its fruit is the talent we possess, something that is inherited and has to be attended to in order to yield a harvest in exchange for money to provide for our survival and comforts in the physical reality.

The Land is the backdrop of our circumstances that provides patterns of experiences related to one of four realms: physical, mental, emotional, or spiritual.

The journey has to be repeated through many lifetimes to undergo the full range of human experiences and achieve the maturity needed for moving to the next, non-earthly plane. In short, the journey is the instruction on finding and claiming one's life purpose through learning hard lessons.

When we break the rules of the Sacred Contract, we may experience health, relationship, or financial problems, called spiritual money blocks. These blocks are not punishments; they make us pause and reexamine our actions as the reminders to get back on track with the Contract.

What can make this journey particularly challenging is the lack of connection with the map that indicates where we need to go and how to get there; however, the possibility of connection is always present. In this context, the challenge is not in just finding the map but being able to connect to the map and interpret it. There are two ways to discover and connect to the map: intuitive and analytical.

Intuitively we often know what we must do in alignment with our purpose because we are guided by a calling. It is this ever-present yet subtle voice that guides us in the actions we must take to satisfy the soul's desire. If the calling is strong, the alignment to purpose becomes natural. Often, it is accompanied by an equally strong gift or talent that must be expressed and put to good use. In this case, the intuitive way may be enough to get us home.

However, frequently the direction itself is not sufficient to get us to the destination. Each Sacred Contract is unique, and each journey is just as unique. I invite you to visit two life stories where a seemingly identical calling could have been the source of misery in each case yet became the story of great success in both.

Two Grand Dames of the Russian Ballet

Anna Pavlova came from humble beginnings and by all accounts should not have been much of a force in the world of ballet. When she graduated from the Russian Imperial Ballet School in the late nineteenth century, her physique and dance style were markedly different from what was considered the *etalon* of the classical dance back then. The ballerinas of her time were plumper yet quite acrobatic. Pavlova, on the other hand was slender and daintier with less physical strength. She was not greeted with warmth and admiration by her peers, to say the least. Yet, blessed with incredible artistic and stage presence, multiplied with endless practice and sharpening her technique, she rose quickly to the rank of a prima ballerina.

She could have easily succumbed to the critique of her appearance, forcing her into trying to fit in and perhaps moving her to the sidelines of the stage. Instead, she tamed what likely was her Dragon—Conformity—by fully stepping into her uniqueness and developing a new style of lyrical dance that won the hearts and accolades of worldwide audiences. She was the first ballerina who performed in all continents and with her own troupe.

Her Castle was the palace of an Artist, and she stepped through its doors by taming her conformity Dragon, located in the land of the Mystics. The role of the Mystics is to serve, as it is the spiritual realm that they occupy. The balance of service is to take care of the self as well as others. Because of her ample gifts, properly nurtured and framed, Pavlova's money flow was abundant. This in turn enabled her to have the lifestyle that was appropriate for a prima ballerina as well as to share the good fortune with those in need. She regularly gave charity concerts with full proceeds going to orphanages.

When the balance of service got tipped—too much service to others through endless performances—it overcame the service to self, and the great ballerina left this world after losing a battle with pneumonia, just weeks before her fiftieth birthday.

A decade her senior, Agripinna Vaganova was another classical dancer who could have taken the wrong turn in navigating the Sacred Contract. Not much historical evidence can be found about the quality and style of her stage performance, perhaps for good reason. While good enough to be on stage and serve at the opera house for nearly twenty years, it appeared that her artistic expression was not particularly remarkable. Her genius, however, was in organizing and systematizing. Singlehandedly she analyzed the three schools of ballet—French, Russian, and Italian—to create a comprehensive syllabus and methodology that is used to this day, nearly one hundred years later, to train classical ballet dancers all over the world. As for the results, Vaganova's method firmly placed the Russian Ballet School as the epitome of classical dance.

It is very likely that Madame Vaganova's Castle was that of a Mentor. Her Dragon probably was The Wrong Work for the Wrong Pay, which she conquered through becoming the methodologist for the Russian Ballet. As a result, she continued serving her beloved art, her nation, and her students well into the mid-twentieth century. Not only had she created a dignified living for herself in the times that were less than plentiful in the newly formed Soviet country, her service influenced the entire world of ballet.

These are historic figures, from another era and the obscure world of dance, and their stories may seem far removed from your life, unless you accept that you, too, have a Sacred Contract. These illustrations can teach each one of us. And if the intuitive way is best served by extraordinary talent and is open to some risk of making the wrong turn, the analytical way would offer you a more direct explanation of what you must do to experience the best version of the life that is meant for you.

To go straight into analysis of your soul map is to decipher the sacred symbols that you carry with you at all times—your fingerprints. Fingerprints form in-utero within three to four months of conception, which is the time that many religions believe the soul enters the body. Remember in The Second Story when Celestial Mother imprinted the Sacred Contract into the children's hands? Your fingerprints are the Sacred Contract. The rest of the hand is the map to your true home and the inventory of your inheritance that you must put to good use.

The following story is from this era and quite inspirational.

Jennifer's Story

With a picture-perfect professional look—manicure, stylish hair, designer dress—Jennifer excitedly sat down and extended her open hands to me, asking for guidance. She wanted to expand her life, write a motivational book, and play big. She listed all her accomplishments, and they were impressive: a family with two high-achieving children, partnership in an accounting firm, community recognition. While her words were painting a story of success, her hands showed something else to me—severe burnout, being boxed in, money blocks. Generally, instead of living in the Castle of a Peaceful Community Leader that she verbalized, it looked like she was deep in the story of a Victim in the Wrong Family. She was puzzled as to why her "successful" life was not giving her the satisfaction she so longed to experience.

In Jennifer's case, it was necessary to tame the Dragon of Guilt by becoming a Mentor—"a life beyond reproach"—in order to open the door to her Castle. That was the stumbling block to her playing big. It's quite amazing how sometimes that one thing can make all the difference in the world.

The Dragon of Guilt is about personal responsibility—with money, obligations, and promises. A Mentor carries responsibility to others not through the words of guidance, but through the acts of personal example. Only having walked her talk would Jennifer get to energetically align to that vibration.

It seemed incredulous that this portrait of perfection would have issues of irresponsibility. And she tried hard to conceal the reality—her marriage was on the rocks, her lifestyle was debt-funded, her professional practice was a conflict of values. No wonder her burnout marks were so deep.

But Jennifer's hands were loaded with gift makers and many positive traits. She understood the cost of keeping the illusion, and she made a choice—not that it came lightly. In just over a year, she ended her marriage, left her practice, and changed her career direction to offer services aligned to her spiritual and healing gifts. And she did write that book with a motivational message, which became a bestseller.

You, too, have a Sacred Contract recorded in your hands. The sacred message of your soul is waiting to be read to help you experience the life that is meant for you—with meaning and prosperity.

Dr. Ollga Belova is the creator of Purpose to Profit Quantum Leap System that helps talented entrepreneurs realize their full life and money potential by overcoming spiritual money blocks.

A former top-level executive, she holds a Doctor of Psychology degree from the California School of Professional Psychology, an MBA from the University of Oxford, Senior HR Professional Certification from SHRM, and number of coaching accreditations, including The Scientific Hand Analysis Certification.

www.OllgaBelova.com

14. FOUR STEPS TO LIVING YOUR LIFE PURPOSE

William Heinrich

If Mark Twain were writing this chapter, this is what he would say: "The two most important days of your life are the day you were born and the day you find out why."

I knew the day I was born, but I began to wonder why. I began my journey as a result of feeling so miserable that I couldn't take it any longer. I was living a life of extreme survival—struggling with low self-esteem, believing that the worst was always yet to come, and perceiving life through judgment, shame, blame, and guilt.

Finally I let go of life as I knew it and changed everything except my name. That was more than twenty-five years ago, and it led to finding the answer to life's biggest questions:

- Why did I come to earth?
- What is the purpose of life?

I wanted to know how it would feel to live 100 percent of the time with passion, purpose, fulfillment, and abundance.

I now know that everyone desires to live this way at some level, but the truth of the matter is that many of us have worked very hard to resolve our life-centered conflicts and yet still aren't getting the answers that feed our souls.

We have been to seminars, purchased programs, and read books, but we still aren't getting the results we desire. The reasons we don't achieve the happiness we are seeking are right before our eyes, but they are so simple that we can't see them. After studying, researching, testing the components of how to live your true life purpose, I now know the reasons happiness is so elusive. I have been coaching people for the past ten years on how to achieve true happiness with a tremendous amount of success.

Life is difficult because we have only been taught to live with a survival mindset. Obviously we need food, water, and shelter to maintain our physical being, or else we will perish. But this mindset, this perception of survival, influences every area of our lives.

A perception of survival causes us to focus on making money, acquiring material things, and achieving goals that will increase our income and improve our physical quality of life. However, the truth of the matter is that new cars, bigger homes, designer clothing, and expensive vacations offer a short-term surge of enjoyment but never allow us to feel truly fulfilled.

A life of survival has certain characteristics that will always appear:

- Developing the ability to hope for the best while always preparing for the worst
- Making decisions from a place of stress and overwhelm
- A focus on lack, supported by a belief that there isn't enough for everyone
- Learning how to endure hardships
- A need to find the lowest price or best deals
- Living in a world of winners and losers
- A perception of making sure we are going to get to death safely

Does this sound familiar?

I lived this way for over forty years . . . until I was so miserable that I couldn't take it anymore. I will share with you the four secrets that I uncovered over the past twenty-five years that permanently ended my misery and have allowed me to constantly live in peace, joy, abundance and freedom.

My promise to you is that these four steps will transform your life and allow you to live a life of passion, purpose, and prosperity. Frankly, I stumbled on every one of these steps by finding out what didn't work. This is key to your success; you must understand the actions—and the results of those actions—that are not taking you toward your purpose. Make a new choice and continue to choose; adjust and choose to go in a new direction.

Four Transformational Steps

1. Understand the difference between surviving and thriving. Surviving will keep you in a constant state of protecting everything and anything in your physical world, from money, security, and material things to the need to create more of them.

Thriving is perception generated from your feelings and is only focused on how you feel and the energy that supports everything you think, say, or do. How you feel is the nonphysical part of life. It is our energy that powers our life purpose. Our energy is what creates everything that manifests into the physical, such as love, gratitude, abundance, passion, and prosperity.

All of our potential and power sits in our nonphysical reality and manifest into our physical world. What you see in the physical is the manifestation of your potential and power. Instead of being limited to your five senses, which provide logic to protect you, it is necessary to tap into your multisensory resources. This how you access intuition, and the more you become aware of these resources, the stronger your intuition becomes.

2. Understand the stories and beliefs that are blocking you, standing in your way, and holding you back. You developed these stories and beliefs as you entered the physical world to survive, but I can assure that they no longer serve you.

We all have these stories and beliefs inside us. The stories are developed through our family of origin and authority figures who have taught us the stories. The majority of these stories are based in a need for protection and control, and they have been passed down through the generations.

You can only experience emotions from your stories. When your stories are focused on protection, the basic emotion you will experience is fear. Examine your stories, buried deep inside you—do they protect you? They may not be serving your highest good any longer.

3. Understand that we are all wearing blinders when it comes making decisions based on who we aren't. We each have individual life lessons that create massive blind spots in our lives, and this is what makes life so challenging. While this is difficult to accept at first, believe me, this is absolutely true. We have each come to earth to learn the lessons that will heal our souls.

Because we have lessons to learn, we have areas in our lives that continually create obstacles, blocks, disruptions, and interruptions in our daily life. The only way to find your path to truth is based on how you feel because your feelings always speak the truth. The stories that support those feelings are probably not true, but how you react to them emotionally gives you an indication of whether or not the stories are serving you in a positive or negative manner.

This is why people will never remember what you said, but they will always remember how you made them feel.

4. Understand that we aren't here to work hard. We each have a very specific Divine Purpose, and when we aren't aware of it, we end up struggling, frustrated, overwhelmed, and stressed out. Our life purpose is not what we are doing in the physical! Our life purpose is created through the energy that fuels every thought, word, and action expressed in our physical life. Our life purpose is not a job description! It is our energy, it is simple, it energizes us and those around us, and it is always expressed for the benefit of all involved in our service to others.

We all come to earth with the same seven Divine Gifts, but everyone has a different proportion of each gift. The Divine Gifts are:

- Divine Compassion—serving others' most basic needs
- Divine Creation—bringing thought into physical form
- Divine Order—an energy of harmony; balance that produces a simple blueprint for actions
- Divine Healing—an energy that makes others feel that they are whole and not broken
- Divine Authentic—words spoken that allow others to create new perceptions; "light bulb" moments
- Divine Truth—an internal knowing of universal truth
- Divine Power—demonstrating the power of choice as it manifests into the physical

These Divine Gifts create our life purpose.

It takes much more energy, struggle, and work when you aren't living your life purpose. As you come to know your life purpose, you have a blueprint that takes you directly to abundance. You will understand the difference between happiness and contentment. Happiness never lasts, while contentment is a foundation of gratitude, trust, and love.

You become ageless and timeless, and life is effortless. You become an energetic magnet that creates unlimited possibilities, momentum, and a blueprint that unleashes infinite opportunities.

We each have a very specific life purpose that we have come to share with others. Our life purpose is so precise that we will always encounter life experiences (in the physical) that will try to disrupt it and take us off our true intended path of being of service to others for the benefit of all involved. As we learn more about our life lessons and make choices that serve our purpose rather than merely focus on physical survival, we create more energetic space that increases our true energetic power.

May you have many blessings on your journey through life!

William Heinrich is a high-level business coach, an executive training director of Scale Pathway, and the author of two books, *The Seven Levels of Truth* and *Clarity Has No Story*. He assists others to discover that the secret of happiness is using the gifts with which the Universe has endowed them.

www.truelifepurposenow.com

15. THE EVOLUTION OF A SOULFUL LEADER

Ronda Renée

The road to soulful leadership can be a long and winding one. There are likely to be many twists and turns before you find yourself on the straight and narrow. Along with the vision to make the world a better place comes volunteering to be the first to walk the path you see for humanity.

That makes this choice to lead one of the most intense personal development courses you will ever enroll yourself in. Understanding the nature of the process will make the long haul ahead much easier and far more enjoyable for you.

No matter where you are on your journey, here are a few things that will be useful to know. First off, while you certainly need some inkling of your purpose in order to start out on the road of soulful leadership, your divine purpose is about more than you may be aware of.

Your purpose isn't actually about what you do. It's not about a project or a mission. And it's definitely not about your business. It's about your own beingness that serves as a greater benefit to the world at large. Each and every person on the planet was born to hold a specific, unique energetic frequency for the world. I call this energetic signature your Divine Coordinates®.

Your Soul has one intention: to master itself. And your Divine Coordinates are the specific pathways it intended to master. This means that there is nothing else on the planet you need to concern yourself with becoming good at. Imagine all the time and energy you could save once you know precisely what you are designed to focus on becoming!

These specific energetic qualities are literally the map of your Soul. Everything in your life is designed to move you closer to the fulfillment of that purpose. This confirms that indeed it will be a journey. The prize is not only in the arrival but in the experience of the journey itself. The more you embody and vibrate with the frequency of your Soul, the more the world receives the gift of you and the more your Divine Contribution is made in the world. In short, your true purpose is not what you *do*—it's who you "be."

Secondly, your mission is as much about you as it is about those you serve—maybe even more so. It's easy to think that your mission is solely about serving others, but in reality, your mission holds the potential of *at least* as much transformation for yourself as it does for those you serve. This is a point that is too often overlooked.

While it may seem as though you started your business to make money while serving others, whether you realize it or not, there is a lot more going on. The truth is that your business is simply the vehicle you've chosen to evolve your own Soul. Others may have chosen parenthood, relationships, or even a physical disability, while for you, it's your business that will offer you the most growth.

If you've chosen the journey of a soulful leader, it means that you will be required to be your own very best client. Along with becoming the embodiment of your Soul's energetic purpose, in order to fulfill your mission, you will be called to become the prime example of your work in the world.

I'm not just talking basic integrity here. Collectively, we are all becoming more and more skillful at sniffing out incongruence and becoming attuned to authenticity and alignment (or the lack thereof). Gone are the days when you could get away with offering something you haven't personally experienced. Walking your talk is no longer optional.

Before you get too worried by that last bit, I hope the final piece I have to share will provide some relief: Where you start is not where you'll finish. As I've said from the start, becoming a soulful leader is a journey. You are far from done yet. I'm not even sure there is a final destination.

When you remember that first, your purpose is about more than what you do and second, your mission is about your own becoming, then you know this path is a process. There will be shifts and changes, adjustments and nudges from the Universe to guide you along the path to your highest service. My own story may help you understand what I mean by this.

Somehow after attending fashion college, I ended up working in construction for over a decade. At the end of my second failed marriage, I took a deep dive into my inner world to sort out what was happening in my life. My own personal inquiry led me to the coaching and training industry, where I immediately felt at home. Without the challenges in my life, I'm not sure how I would have known that I could consider a career in personal development. But as it turns out, my journey was only just getting started.

My first foray into coaching and training was leading emotional authenticity workshops for teenagers. It just so happened that I had two of my own at the time and about a dozen others that called me Mom even though they weren't technically mine. While I loved leading those workshops, I was repeatedly frustrated at having only one day to work with these teenagers, so I started adding private coaching to my practice.

My next frustration came from working so hard to empower these teens only to send them back into disempowering environments. That's when I added parent coaching to my teen coaching. The only way I would agree to coach a teen was to also coach at least one of the parents. I have to say, it was fun to teach parents quantum physics principles such as the "observer effect" in order to improve their relationships with their kids. But my path didn't stop there.

Most of time the parent I ended up coaching was the mom—although I did have this awesome farmer dad who used to call me for his session from his tractor parked right in the middle of his field! It just so happened that I had been a single mother for about eight years at this point. I'd previously had a very demanding sales career, so I understood overwhelm. I had also been a master at managing it. People would frequently ask me, "How are you doing all this?" Back then my answer was "I don't know; I'm just doing it!"

Looking back I could see exactly how I did it. So I created my first group coaching program called *Transform Your To-Do List: From Overwhelmed to Overjoyed.* That went really well and was super fun! But guess what? You got it! I wasn't done yet.

The fact is that once someone gets out of overwhelm, they start asking bigger questions, and ultimately that almost always leads to wanting to know what all the busyness is even about. They want to know what their purpose is. They want to know why they're here. That's where Divine Navigation® and Divine Coordinates® came in.

If I hadn't been willing to allow my purpose to lead me and my mission to change and expand, I would never have ended up here today. Luckily, something bigger than me knew better than me.

From the outside, it was in no way obvious where all this was leading me. But when I let go of the wheel and let my Soul navigate, I ended up exactly where I was meant to be. That young gal who had always dreamed of working in fashion in New York City could never have imagined that this is what she was meant to do with her life!

On your path of soulful leadership, you can be certain you will be course-corrected and redirected—multiple times—along the way. That doesn't mean you aren't on the right path. (Well, OK, sometimes you aren't.) You might simply be on a necessary detour to gather the skills, insights, and resources you'll need to prepare you to fulfill your divine purpose. Either way, it's always a more successful journey when you have the right map—the map of your Soul!

Ronda Renée, founder of Divine Navigation® and creator of the Divine Coordinates® process, has led thousands to success through alignment with their Soul. Ronda guides business leaders and entrepreneurs in running the business their Soul wants them to run so they can make the difference and the money they were meant to make.

www.DivineNavigation.com

16. CHOOSING THE BENEFICIAL

Monique D. Toh

I wrote and illustrated a story on sticky notes when I was a child. The story was about a princess who gets lost in a dense forest and her crown falls off. Lost and confused, she is surprised to when a little monkey comes up to her. She tells the monkey that she is lost and has lost her crown. Nodding with understanding and an idea, the monkey sets off to find the crown. When the monkey returns with the crown, the princess gratefully places the crown upon her head. Feeling confident again, she soon finds her way out of the forest. The story ends with a ceremony celebrating the little monkey who proved to be a faithful friend.

In yoga lore, there is a monkey god named Hanuman who is known to illuminate illusion. In the epic story of the *Ramayana*, Hanuman is Rama's most loyal servant and helps Rama and Sita out of many scrapes. Before Hanuman became so helpful, he had been a small, naughty monkey who fell prey to a curse that caused him to forget all of his powers. Once he hustled to remove the curse, Hanuman remembered all of his dynamic, divine powers. His legendary powers included both transforming himself into the size of a mountain and flying across a sea channel. In fact, there is a yoga pose named after him called *Hanumanasana* that depicts the splits as he flies across the ocean.

In many ways, I also felt cursed as a child. I had a tough childhood with many difficult aspects. There was neglect, abuse, poverty, and addiction all around me.

Growing up around addiction, it is quite easy to absorb the up-and-down energy cycles that go with it. Many people continue those roller-coaster cycles for themselves as adults. For me, I found a widely available drug to continue the pattern of ups and downs: food. Though I didn't know it until my mid-thirties, I had a binge eating disorder, and I regularly numbed my anxieties and feelings with food. Eating like this plunged me into guilt, weight problems, and insecurity. I lost my "crown," the knowledge of my true value and self-worth. Growing up around dysfunction convinced me of my own worthlessness.

The turning point began when I came across the books of a meditation and yoga master, with whom I later had an opportunity to meet and study. This teacher turned out to be my "Hanuman" who set me on a new path of healing, recovery, and the rebuilding of self-worth. One meditation, one yoga practice, and one meal at a time, I was able to heal my eating disorder and find inner stability and peace.

A helpful yoga teaching that I have learned is to choose the *Shreyas* (beneficial in the long-term) over the *Preyas* (pleasurable in the short-term). Practicing discipline to keep making beneficial adjustments in my lifestyle and activities helps me to deepen my worthiness and to experience more stability and fewer ups and downs. So, rather than sleeping in, most days I make it a point to sit for early morning meditation, which plants the seeds of tranquility in my day. Rather than leaving myself open to eating foods that make my blood sugar chemically imbalanced, I eat a delicious plant-based diet that keeps me trim and untriggered by food. Rather than eating lots of tasty, fried, and salty snacks that interfere with digestion and sabotage my meals, I try to fill my belly at mealtimes with yummy dishes consisting of whole grains, lentils, beans, vegetables, fruits, nuts, seeds, and warming spices. Over time, I've also cut out caffeine and alcohol by choosing what would help me in the long run over momentary experiences of pleasure or trying to fit in "socially."

Although it may seem that choosing the beneficial over the pleasurable sounds like a dull life of discipline and drudgery, actually the opposite is true. Setting reasonable goals and limits with ourselves sets us up for self-esteem-building success. We learn to trust ourselves and to shed negative habits that no longer serve us. This is an expansive experience of freedom.

Choosing the beneficial goes beyond food and drink. Technology is something that we could all use some help with in choosing the beneficial over the pleasurable. Perhaps instead of reaching for our phones first thing in the morning, we could set aside five to fifteen minutes to read something uplifting, journal, pray, or meditate before starting the day. A few minutes of quality self-care in the morning goes a long way in ensuring that we have a positive mindset for the day.

I have a yoga lifestyle coaching practice. One of my clients, Nora, found that during the pandemic with all of her family home, she was spending the majority of her morning hours wasting time on her phone. Taking care of her home and her family started to feel like a draining chore, and she herself felt increasingly lost. She decided to choose the beneficial over the pleasurable and shifted her morning to be about connecting to herself and to God. Now, after she wakes up, she takes her coffee and sits on her yoga mat. She reads the Quran. Once she finds an inspiring verse, she takes an old-fashioned fountain pen with traditional Indian ink and paints a few words in Arabic. With her creativity flowing freely, she moves into about thirty minutes of practicing yoga. Her mornings have turned into an important ritual that generates spiritual connectedness and enthusiasm that fuel her days.

Another client recently had an interesting choice to make about technology. Hannah was in a romantic relationship that clearly needed to end. After their third attempt at breaking up, she found that she could not stop checking Instagram to look at her ex's posts. It was making her miserable, yet she was compelled to keep fiddling with the remaining strings that bound them together. Finally, she chose herself and her sanity and unfriended her ex on all platforms. She decided to cut the strings of texting him and keeping tabs on his social media. She chose the beneficial thing. Although it took time to recover from the breakup, she found herself truly happy in the long run.

How will you know how to choose *Shreyas* over *Preyas* in your life? Listening to therapists, teachers, experts, finding inspiration in books and online, and hearing anecdotes from friends can give provide hints and clues. But ultimately it is up to each of us to listen to ourselves, our bodies, and our feelings for the signs and directions we could follow. It is a long, trial-and-error experiment to continue to choose things that will benefit us in the long run. Luckily, we have our whole lives to keep putting our "crowns" back on and find our way out of forest after forest in order to experience long-term rewards such as spiritual healing, vibrant health, and inner peace.

Monique D. Toh is a yoga lifestyle coach with twenty-five years of yoga and teaching experience. Monique holds a MA from Rice University and a certification in plant-based nutrition from Cornell. She lives in Houston, Texas, where she offers online nutrition workshops, yoga classes for adults, kids, and seniors, life-coaching, and yoga retreats.

www.YogicDiet.com

17. SEVEN WORDS TO LIVE BY

Nancy Fields

Any work that is born out of natural serendipity or reverts to simpler times is poignant for people—in any era.

—Cai Guo-Qiang

Have you ever said, "I have always wanted to do that"?

In the mid-1970s, a friend told me that his mother was a stay-at-home mom who designed greeting cards for Hallmark.

I would love to do that! At the time, I was in college; another year of tests and exams were staring at me. Although the desire was strong, I did not say it out loud. Nor did I take any action for the next twenty-five years.

One day while visiting an artist studio, a small framed piece caught my attention.

"What's that?" I inquired with great interest.

"It's calligraphy."

"I have always wanted to do that!"

Shifting from thoughts of *I would love to do that* to declaring "I have always wanted to do that!" was the spark that led me down a path I could never have imagined.

I was now a stay-at-home mom with two small children under the age of five.

Soon I enrolled in my first calligraphy class. Being able to sit quietly for one hour was heaven. The six weeks flew by.

In my second calligraphy class, a fellow student brought in a design she was sending off to Hallmark the following day. It was exciting to see her original calligraphy and watercolor illustration carefully packaged for shipping.

That night, all I could think about was learning how to reproduce my calligraphy.

I met with a graphic design instructor at a local community college, showed him my work, and told him I wanted to design greeting cards. He suggested I take a class in Photoshop and one in graphic design.

By this time my youngest son was in preschool, my oldest in kindergarten. The timing was perfect. I could take classes while they were in school.

My First Client

The invitation read: "Come to view a line of women's clothing at my home at 11:00 a.m."

An hour before my appointment, I decided to practice my calligraphy.

The phone rang.

The bottle of black ink tipped over and spilled all over my hands.

Soap and water would not remove the ink that was now deep under my fingernails.

Upon arriving, I apologized for my appearance and assured the woman that my ink-stained hands would not soil her beautiful dresses.

"You do calligraphy?"

"Yes."

"Do you also design invitations?"

Many invitations and thousands of hand-calligraphed envelopes later, my design studio was in full bloom.

This same customer took a fundraising job at a private school. She soon needed invitations—plus brochures, pamphlets, a catalogue, event signage, and logos. I was her go-to person for all things "creative."

Over the next fifteen years, other schools and colleges, small museums, and private practice owners requested my graphic design services. My signature "mark" was hand calligraphy combined with traditional graphic design.

My business grew so rapidly that I hired freelance designers, a part-time office assistant, and a bookkeeper . . . until 2008 when the stock market crashed.

Am I Still in Business?

By 2008, many businesses had moved online, and beautiful hand-rendered fonts were ubiquitous. Offset printers were feeling the pinch too. One printing company I hired for all of my "schools work" went to two of my best customers. The printer convinced my customers he could save them money by designing and printing in-house whatever they needed.

I had become the middleman. The printers had all my job files, meaning they could design and print whatever my customers wanted and needed in the look they were accustomed to.

It was a strange time. I went from outputting 130 print jobs a year to twelve.

The phone stopped ringing.

I let my last employee go and wondered if this was the end of my design business.

I signed up for another calligraphy class with a new instructor who was also an illustrator. Mary created ornate wedding certificates, certificates of appreciation, and book illustrations—all by hand.

Much to my surprise, I never said, "I have always wanted to do that!" when I saw Mary's beautiful work, but I did say, "I have always wanted to create my own alphabet!"

Two New Words

Create plus *alphabet*—two words that would inspire action and allow me to combine all the things the Universe heard me say I had always wanted to do.

Monogram stationery was my project name. It spanned thousands of years of words on paper. In fourth-century tradition, my letters were rendered by hand and illuminated in 18K gold leaf. I added botanical drawings.

Using modern technology, my original artwork was scanned. Once in my computer, I enhanced and edited the illustrations, but the brilliant gold letters lost their sparkle. Like diamonds, gold leaf needs light to show off its beauty. Foil stamping was too costly. So, using my Photoshop skills, the dull gold was replaced with a color that complimented the illustration.

Designing a gift box to hold the notecards was a challenge because boxes are printed flat before they are assembled. Thanks to years of bookbinding classes, paper folding, and creating one-off artists books, I was not deterred from designing a box template to fit ten envelopes and ten notecards. But this meant I first had to choose the paper before calculating the height and width of the box. Thank goodness algebra and basic math always had seemed fun to me.

My customers who loved high-end stationery always insisted on lined envelopes for privacy. Instead of having envelopes lined, paper was printed on one side and sent off to the envelope fabricator—another cost savings.

My notecards still needed to be printed, but my print run was too small for a large four-color printing press. Fortunately a new technology had emerged for jobs like mine: high-quality, four-color printing on a digital press.

Five Words That Spark Desire

The first time I recall saying "I'd love to do that!" was when I was five years old and walked into my kindergarten classroom.

Easels were set up in the back. I rushed over and grabbed a large wooden brush. The bristles were soft and thick.

Sixty years later, I can still remember the smell of the water-based paints tucked into the easel tray. A fresh sheet of newsprint was begging for my masterpiece.

In a flash I was sitting in first grade—in a different classroom, but day after day at the same desk, in the same row, surrounded by the same forty-five classmates.

The only break in this routine was a weekly visit from the penmanship teacher. She was younger than my first grade teacher, and as beautiful as her perfectly formed letters.

With a hypnotic gaze, my eyes fixed on her rake-like tool as she inserted four new pieces of chalk into each metal holder. Ruler positioned, she drew equally spaced white lines across the freshly washed slate board. Then she demonstrated how to create our letters.

With sharpened pencils on specially lined paper, it was our turn to practice our handwriting. My own letters were praised by this goddess. I could hardly wait to get home to show my mother.

I don't recall visits from the penmanship instructor in second grade, but I do remember the taste of paste and our bimonthly visits from the art teacher. She was petite, donned a cherry red barrette, and always seemed happy to see us. It was a sharp contrast to our everyday teacher who wore heavy leg braces and slapped her cane on the floor—and on anything else that irritated her—as she lumbered to her desk.

Years would pass before the words *school* and *I have always wanted to do that* were uttered in the same breath. It seemed that the opportunity to be creative was replaced with addition, subtraction, reading, science, French, and taking tests.

Today, though, when those seven magical words roll off my tongue, I have learned to pay attention and take action to see what's next.

What causes you to say, "I have always wanted to do that"?

Nancy Fields is a graphic designer, web designer, calligrapher, and botanical illustrator. She feels truly blessed to have grown up with an aunt who was blind. That experience encouraged her to describe what she saw in greater detail and to appreciate the gift of sight.

www.FieldsGraphicDesign.com

18. SOULFUL LEADERSHIP AND THE FORCES OF LOVE, HOPE, AND BREAKTHROUGH

Dr. Melissa Andersson

I will never forget it. Two little six-year-old girls were laughing and playing. A car that had been parked up the hill was rolling toward them, and they never saw it coming. A man jumped in front of the moving car and tried to stop it.

Eventually he bridged himself between the car parked on the lower side of the hill and the vehicle that was about to crush the little girls. They slipped out beneath him just in time.

I was one of the little girls, and the man was my dad.

The neighbors were watching in horror from their porches but couldn't get to us in time. It was a tradition in our little town that the parents would come out on the porches in the late afternoon and watch the kids playing in the streets. Each street like ours was marked with street signs that read "Children Playing."

My dad, by all logic, was not physically able to hold off a thousand pounds of rolling vehicle. The event sparked a lot of conversations throughout the neighborhood and town. It seemed that everyone had a secret story that they never talked about regarding moments of superhuman strength and miraculous healings.

They all knew stories of moms and dads lifting cars off of their children who were pinned underneath due to an accident. According to the buzz, ordinary people could do extraordinary things.

This may have been the starting point that has led me on a lifelong journey of exploring human potential.

Eventually, Mom and Dad divorced. Mom and I moved far away from the supportive community of our little town. When I was twelve years old, Mom remarried. A few days after the wedding, Mom was hospitalized with what the doctors called a life-threatening strain of flu. I was afraid that she would die.

I was also sick with this flu. I was extremely weak, lying in bed, and throwing up in a garbage can.

Mom's new husband came home and demanded that I come out of the bedroom. I responded through the door, "I'm sick, I'm throwing up, and I'm dizzy. I'm not dressed."

The man broke the flimsy lock on my bedroom door and dragged me out of bed. As I stood there in panties and a T-shirt, he demanded that I go to the kitchen and cook his dinner.

"I can't," I said. "I'm too sick."

Then he chased me around the house. When he caught me, he threw me on the hard dining room floor and jumped on top of me.

I was shocked and terrified. No man had ever done this to me before. I was a tiny and petite child—probably around four feet, five inches tall and weighing less than eighty pounds. My mind raced. Was he going to rape me? I screamed out for someone to come and help me. He stopped my screams by putting his hand over my mouth and nose. I couldn't breathe. I thought I was going to die.

I felt helpless. I thought of my mom lying in the hospital in a very serious condition that could lead to her death. I thought that if she recovered and found out that I had died, my precious mom would be forever devastated beyond measure.

Then something happened. Was it my pleading prayers or the powerful love that I had for my mother? A force seemed to come over me, and a strength arose in me. I managed to get the man off my body.

After that incident, I felt as though my life was over. The man didn't succeed in raping me, but he seemed to have an agenda to destroy my soul—to break me into believing that I was worthless and that he had an inalienable right to put me in servitude to do his bidding.

I had always done well in school, but that year I barely had enough attendance to pass. I developed migraines and horrible intestinal problems. My mom worked nights at the hospital, which left me alone with the man during the night. I didn't dare fall asleep.

As I look back, I know that I was suffering from clinical depression and Post Traumatic Stress Disorder. I was terrified to tell anyone what happened. The man told me that if I did, he would kill my mom. I prayed and prayed for help and strength. I prayed that I could find peace in my heart and my traumatized brain. Many times I contemplated committing suicide, but every time I came close, I thought about how devastated my mom would be.

In subsequent years, I learned that a great many children were suffering terribly from psychological and sexual abuse. As young teens, we formed an unofficial underground railroad of sorts. Often, with the help of parents who were mental health professionals, we strategize ways to help kids cope or escape to a "safe house." Every one of those dedicated parents and kids were soulful leaders. It was unacceptable to let young lives be destroyed. I'm so grateful for what we were able to do.

At age sixteen, the state's mental health authority certified me to counsel on the teen and adolescent suicide hotlines as a suicide and crisis counselor. Providing that service was heart-wrenching, but I could speak from a place deep in my heart since I, too, once thought that death was the only way to escape my pain. I was grateful to be alive and also grateful that I could help others and give them hope.

When I was twenty-two, I went to work on cruise ships. That leap of faith led me to explore much of the world: the Caribbean, South and Central America, Europe, Alaska, Australia, the Pacific Islands, and places as remote as Papua New Guinea. Oh, the adventures were amazing!

I made up for some of the time I lost in my childhood. I felt a great sense of joy, freedom, and exhilaration. I did things I never had the opportunity to do before. I learned to sail small sailboats and scuba dive in some of the most beautiful waters of the world. Having never ridden a horse before, I felt a oneness with the horses I met who loved to run full-out in wild abandon on remote beaches. I learned to make short documentary films and silly movies with my crew member friends.

More importantly, I was able to see soulful leadership in its many forms. I got to know international leaders, celebrities, and conscientious corporate leaders. I visited some of the most elegant places in the world, but also some of the poorest.

Soulful leadership is many things in many forms. It's honesty, integrity, compassion, and the commitment to lift up lives in a family, a neighborhood, a company, a country, or the world.

I believe that my crewmates and I carried out soulful leadership when we sought to uplift people wherever we went. Sometimes it was just reaching out with a smile or a gesture—an acknowledgment that no matter how poor people were, they mattered as humans to us. Sometimes we could do more with community donations and by helping to create pathways to employment or the creation of small businesses and co-ops.

After some years, it was time for me to come ashore and explore more in the areas of human potential. From the time I was a child, I never stopped reading books to help me understand the meaning of life, how to move through sadness and bring it to joy, and how to heal the deepest wounds of the human psyche.

One of my first trainings led to certification in advanced hypnotherapy. My instructor was considered one of the "old masters" and the consummate expert on the subconscious and super-conscious mind. He advocated "regression to cause" as the most powerful way to release issues at their core. In my practice, there was hardly a day that I wasn't in awe of the power of the human mind. I soon studied many modalities in the fields of energy medicine and energy psychology that allowed me to track root causes (traumas, self-defeating belief systems, abundance blocks, etc.) in moments and clear them quickly.

Yet I also longed for ways to help people reach higher levels of energy that would help them step forward in healing and life. I was working with several cancer patients at the time on the emotional aspects of illness. A lot of them were depleted and felt paralyzed. Many of them felt alone and helpless. I wanted to help them raise their energy and give them experiences of love, laughter, play, and joy. I wanted to offer breakthrough experiences to help them feel more empowered.

As a result, I soon found myself on a mountaintop in Italy. For weeks I was immersed in a deeply intensive program of certified firewalk instructor training. Every day we were raising our vibrations, creating a sense of community and trust, and breaking through to do "the impossible." By day we broke arrows at our throats, walked barefoot on broken glass, and did angel walks and trust exercises. We paired up with partners to bend rebar at our throats (i.e., "bending steel with our hearts"). By night we danced on hot burning coals.

It's been my joy to help people courageously step through fear and perceived limitations—laughing, joyous, and in awe of their own capacities. What I hear people say most often is, "If I can do this, what more can I do?"

I am grateful for all the soulful leaders we have in this world. They embody all skills, all backgrounds, and all areas of focus. Some have come through very hard times to get where they are today, but they never gave up. Together they weave a beautiful tapestry that makes a tremendously positive difference in the world!

Dr. Melissa Andersson is a positive breakthrough specialist, trained in a multitude of modalities from Energy Psychology to Firewalk Instructor. She facilitates interactive seminars that set people on a quantum course of the "Human Possible," laughing, joyous, and in awe of their own capacities.

www.HumanPotentialCentral.com

19. TRANSFORMING YOUR STORY INTO YOUR STAND

Iman Khan

It had been about eighteen months since we all watched in horror as the towers came down, since we watched people screaming as the ash outran them and blacked out the city in broad daylight—and since we watched those poor people jump from windows rather than burn alive.

These are images I've lived with and have never been able to purge from my mind since they were imprinted there on that fateful day. So, when President Bush announced that we were invading Iraq, and the subsequent death that instantly equaled in my mind, I became unable to stay silent any longer.

As far as I can remember, I've always stood up for people. Watching people be picked on or bullied was something I could never tolerate. I grew up one of three kids of color in my elementary school and one of five in middle school and high school. Getting picked on and bullied was an everyday event for us, even though I was well-liked and had a ton of friends. In fact, it was often those friends who bullied me, but I was confident about not having to face consequences if I stood up for others.

When we'd visit Bangladesh as a child, it was all I could do to free my family's servants from what I saw as unjust. Not because my family mistreated them, but because of their station in life. I'd sneak the rickshaw drivers extra money or get caught in growing mobs of people looking for handouts because I would just start handing out money to anyone I could. Standing up for those who can't defend themselves is part of my DNA.

This changed after 9/11. I was on the F-Train coming back to Queens from the West Village when three women attacked a young Muslim woman and began to rip her hijab off. When I heard them say, "You fu**ing Muslim," I intervened and got between them and the young lady. Those three women instantly transferred their rage to me, and I'd never been slapped or kicked so many times in my life. I covered my face and took the hits. I also stopped saying anything to anyone.

Every time I wanted to stand up for someone after that subway incident, I held myself back— until I watched Bush announce the US invasion of Iraq.

I knew he was lying about WMD. I'd studied to become a journalist and had extensively studied history. I had also researched Dick Cheney and Karl Rove by then and knew they were lying, and I felt gutted. Right away, maybe because I'm an empath, I began to feel all the suffering Iraqis would go through as a result of the invasion of their homes.

Seventeen years later, over a million dead, the rise of dozens of terror groups that hadn't existed before, a nation torn apart, history decimated, resources looted, and the region completely destabilized—I felt the reality of it all in that moment, and after eighteen months of being silent in a way I had never before been silent, I thought I'd explode.

That weekend was the first of many trips to D.C. to protest the war. I began protesting everywhere I could, whenever I could. That declaration of war against Iraq was my "never again" moment, and ever since, much of my life has been designed around speaking up—and more importantly, empowering as many people as I possibly can to also take a stand. To speak up and use their voice for good. To stand up for people who can't stand up for themselves.

This has not been an easy road. When I was involved in the Palestinian/Israeli conflict, my loved ones (as well as Palestinian and Israeli friends) told me I had no business in that fight. When I worked near Penn Station, I'd frequently get into it with police who were arresting and sometimes abusing our city's homeless population who had nowhere else to go. During the #metoo movement, when I posted about my own sexual abuse, I got hate mail from more women that I could count, again telling me that this wasn't my fight because I was a male. Recently, as I vocalized my thoughts and experiences around COVID-19, even after suffering personal loss, I've been vilified by people. As a South Asian man, I've been actively posting about the Black Lives Matter movement on my social media channels for almost seven years, and nothing I've participated in has met with more vitriol, hate, or resistance.

Yet with every ounce of resistance I'm met with, my heart breaks, and my resolve fortifies. Here's what I've learned since 2003: no matter what people's views are and no matter how wrong or right those views seem to others, people want to stand for something. They want purpose, and they want to make a difference. Sometimes it's for their family or friends, sometimes for their colleagues or their neighborhood or even the world—but the drive to make a difference seems universal.

I've also discovered that turning a blind eye never works. It's destructive to people, to society, to the world, and most of all, to our individual spirits.

The rationalizations we have to invent in our minds to be OK with looking the other way diminish our understanding of ourselves and of how to live out our respective purposes. Life becomes about having to manage our reduced understanding of what we're capable of and justifying that. These justifications then spill into every part of our lives, and suddenly all we have are mediocre, unsatisfying lives that we then have to hide behind various facades that protect our new and reduced life narratives.

All it leads to is masking from the world that we don't feel whole. For introverts, this often leads to isolation, whereas extroverts often try to prove how wonderful their lives are via social media or some other form of pretense that gives their personalities the dopamine hits they need whenever getting a like or a comment on some platform or another.

Confronting things feels a lot harder and seems so much riskier—but that discomfort is temporary, and the reward for confronting what scares us is far richer and more satisfying than the temporary relief of turning away.

Watching someone you respect, admire, or even love transform their views and get free of whatever was holding them back because you refused to turn away—especially when it gets tough—makes everything worth it.

The heartache, the tears, the pain, and the stress all melt away in the moments when that type of transformation takes place.

Iman Khan has been on a mission to impact the world in a positive way since childhood, and in 2011 he and his wife, Afrin, launched Red Elephant, which empowers entrepreneurs to go beyond their comfort zone to reach their goals and achieve massive success along the way.

www.RedElephantInc.com

20. FROM INVISIBLE TO IMPACT

Afrin Khan

Has there ever been a moment when you've asked yourself, "Is this all there is to my life, or is there something bigger for me to pursue?"

I think there is a calling within each of us—a desire for our lives to be bigger than this.

I remember at an early age feeling this call to make my mark in the world, likely because my family was academically exceptional. My mother was the first to go to college in her village in Bangladesh. She completed her master's degree and became a successful anatomy and cell biologist at SUNY Downstate Medical Center. My father was a PhD in Cataloguing Science, became a librarian at St. John's University, and wrote several reference books. My brother graduated from Yale University and is currently working at Google.

And then there is me, Afrin. I wanted to be and do something big in the world. But I was always stopped by:

I am female.
I am a person of color.
I am a Muslim.
And my name is also a well-known nasal spray.

When I thought about meeting new people and speaking up or being a leader, my brain used to quickly kick into survival mode. *Afrin, YOU'RE SCREWED. Who is going to listen to you?*

How could I make it big when I couldn't even overcome the reaction to my name, let alone own who I am as a Muslim woman of color?

That noisy voice in my head would shout, *Afrin, stop thinking about living a life bigger than what you can handle. You won't be able to survive.*

Then I did what many twenty-somethings do. I moved to San Diego and got a job. If I was going to struggle to survive, I wanted to do it with a view! I moved in with two roommates near a private beach in town called Leucadia. I landed a well-paying corporate marketing job that I loved. I bought a sports car with a stick shift and zipped up and down the coast of California, or down to Rosarito, Mexico, or even to Las Vegas during my weekends and downtime when I wasn't working.

I finally felt like I was living the life.

But the question I continued to wrestle with, the one that kept gnawing at me, was: "Is this all there is to my life, or is there something bigger for me to pursue?" As timing would have it, my brother invited me to participate in a three-day transformational training that promised to answer two seemingly unanswerable questions: "Who am I?" and "What is my life for?"

During those three days, I had many moments of clarity, but the insights that hit me over the head like a two-by-four are the ones that would put me on the path to discover my calling and make the impact I've always wanted to make.

Yes, I am a Muslim woman of color with an uncommon name. That doesn't mean I have to play small and be invisible in the world. I can create who I am beyond my race, religion, and gender.

I made a choice to play a big game and challenge those barriers that once intimidated me. And I continued to challenge myself every step of the way.

Making that choice didn't suddenly solve all my problems or provide me with a direct path to success. In fact, there have been twists and turns regularly along the way, but that's a chapter for another book.

The real eye-opener is understanding that to move from invisible to impact is a lot like giving birth. You have an idea to create something new—maybe it's an idea of how you can reinvent yourself. You incubate on the idea. There is a gestation period. There is a period of questioning, self-doubt, and hesitation. You go through a process of validation from yourself and others. You start having confidence in yourself to go through with it. There is no going back. You have drawn a line in the sand. You have made the announcement. And now you and others are looking forward to seeing the new creation. For some the birth is painful; for others it's effortless. Once born, you know to focus your attention on nurturing and protecting your new creation. You hope people don't judge, criticize, or think it's ugly. You hope *you* won't think it's ugly!

As with all births, the transformation from invisible to visible emerges through a long and sometimes painful process.

This story has now become my stand, my purpose, my torch to light up the way for others who are seeking guidance on how to make an impact in the world.

The first client of ours who broke through the barriers of being invisible, Re Perez of Branding For The People, now has a multimillion-dollar company serving the top entrepreneurs worldwide. Our vision expanded and now we serve a diverse community of entrepreneurs who are committed to making a difference in the world, including Mark Porteous, Jan Edwards, Allyson Byrd, Steve Olsher, Kim Butler, Monica Shah, Shameca Tankerson, Pia Silva, Danielle Posa, and Deepak Chopra.

Once invisible, now I make an impact. I no longer sit on the sidelines. I am seen. I am heard. I lead by example. I continually expand, explore, and take risks. I nurture others, all who are grounded in a commitment to transformation and making a difference. I am known for impacting thousands of leaders, entrepreneurs, and visionaries to be a force in the marketplace.

Now that I'm on the other side of breaking through being invisible and making an impact, I realize that one question never really goes away . . . it's how you show up in response to it:

"Is this all there is to my life, or is there something bigger for me to pursue?"

For over twenty years, **Afrin Khan** has guided individuals, groups, and corporations around the world to produce breakthrough results in the areas of speaking, leadership, and making an impact. She is renowned for cultivating an extraordinary, collaborative community of change agents and for pioneering cutting-edge training methods and techniques.

www.RedElephantInc.com

21. THE MIRACULOUS POWER OF VIBRATION AND FREQUENCY

Barry Auchettl

If you want the answers to the universe,
think in terms of energy, vibration, and frequency.
—*Nicola Tesla*

"You have two hours left to live," I was told in 2008 when I was hospitalized with a blood clot to my brain. The sequence of events in my life over the last twenty-five years is not nearly as important as who I have become now.

Twenty-five years ago, I was an educator, teaching accounting, computers, and religion. Primarily, I was "asleep" and lived my life to provide food for my family and pay the mortgage.

Then the most extraordinary set of events occurred. I first spent six months getting out of multi-focal glasses after wearing them for over fifteen years. I did this by experimenting on myself with various processes to improve my eyesight. A week after completing 20/20 on an eye chart, though, I was diagnosed with a pituitary tumor sitting on the optic nerve. Two weeks later I was operated on for over five hours.

The changes in my life over the next few years were immense. I refused an operation to remove a second tumor that would have left me on medication for life and instead embarked on a journey of self-help and conscious development.

I started by creating a business called Eye Power that supports people in improving their own eyesight as well as gaining greater insights into their lives. Next I created a collaborative board game called *Conversations*, an inspirational game that enables people to communicate, engage, and connect with one another.

I also established a kinesiology business working with individual clients and teaching groups of people how to muscle test. While there was a large degree of personal development in all of these endeavors, my own life appeared to deteriorate. In 2008, I had to undergo a second brain operation to remove the remaining tumor, and the result was a blood clot that developed a week later. That same year my wife and I decided to separate, and I was isolated amongst my closest friends in the city where I grew up.

A new relationship and a new place to live helped create a new spark in my life. Yet six years later, I found myself alone again, with all three of my businesses showing promise but no real substantial financial return.

I needed a change in my life that supported the internal changes I had experienced. I felt as though I had done so much inner work, yet my new life had not yet shown up fully. So, for my 2015 New Year's resolution, I created a process for myself that I planned to undertake for thirty days to try and create a real miracle in my life.

By the end of January, I had accepted a keynote speaking engagement for the International Vision Educators' conference in Los Angeles to be held in May. On top of this, I had greater support from my friends than I'd had in years.

The success of this particular personal experiment meant that I decided to continue the process again for the next month. By the end of February, I had organized a five-month world tour to ten countries—a once-in-a-lifetime plan to travel fully around the world.

I have continued this particular thirty-day process ever since. Each month, new and incredible miracles have occurred in my life. Over the past twelve months, I've met amazing people who have inspired me and allowed me to inspire them. This has included a new relationship of great depth that has enabled me to feel part of a family again.

During the process of traveling the world, I managed to connect with some incredible people who helped raise my own personal vibration and level of consciousness. Each person seemed to appear from nowhere in order to support this change as I developed new levels of consciousness beyond what I thought was possible.

Then, at the beginning of 2016, I started to explore the differences between an individual vibrational rate and the subsequent frequency we radiate out to attract the things we want in life. I found that although the two are often similar, they might not necessarily be calibrating at the same rate. I also found that when you lift your own personal vibrational rate, it stays at the new calibrated rate despite what is happening in your life. The frequency we radiate can, however, be moved up and down and be affected by such things as emotions, stress, sleep patterns, beliefs, and sabotages.

I often get asked to explain the difference between vibration and frequency. I distinguish between the two by saying that vibration relates to our own personal level of consciousness, whereas frequency relates to the external Law of Attraction.

The level of consciousness we have relates to our own connection to spirit. As such, meditation is the best way of increasing our vibrational state. As we raise our own personal vibration, life takes on different meanings and opportunities for miracles to occur. As we raise our own personal vibration, it supports the frequency we are putting out to the world. Thus, your intent should be to increase both your internal vibration and your external frequency.

Raising Your Vibration and Your Frequency

Each one of us vibrates at a certain level. Our vibration is directly related to our levels of consciousness, whereas our frequency is the connection between ourselves and the world. The higher your frequency, the more you're able to connect to others on a deeper level, and the further your frequency will reach in the world. This is more than just luck. Luck is the physical manifestation from raising your frequency. What appears lucky is simply an echo of the Law of Attraction where vibrations match the same frequency.

The idea is to match the frequency of what you're after to your own personal frequency. For example, if you are looking for a new home, ideally you would want to match the frequency of your new home with your own frequency. This will enable that home to come into your awareness more quickly.

The best way to increase your frequency is through gratitude. The more grateful you are for what is in your life, the more quickly you can raise your frequency. Another way to increase your frequency is to meditate or even hang out with other people with higher frequencies. Groups of people tend to operate at a higher frequency than any of the individuals within the group, so group dynamics help to raise the energy and frequencies of everyone in the room. This is where miracles can occur for all those present.

A combination of these processes brings more joy and balance into your life, especially if you add the virtues of mindfulness, creativity, appreciation, and wonder. The result is that you get to create miracles and step into and live your life's purpose with ease and grace.

Raising your vibration is a journey and not a destination. There is no limit to the potential of your uniqueness here on this planet. Even if you reached infinity, you would find that there were powers of infinity that you could explore.

There is nothing like seeing the results for yourself to encourage you to continue. Miracles that have come up for me have included deeper relationships, more financial freedom, and being asked to speak around the world. The biggest miracle of all was being told by a neurosurgeon that my brain tumor was gone, and he didn't want to see me again.

Where to from Here?

If you're ready to move beyond the glass ceiling you have created, begin taking personal responsibility for your own life and consider working with a program that will allow you to raise your personal vibration (inner consciousness) and your frequency in the world (outer manifestation) on a daily basis. You no longer need to do this by yourself and can be supported by a dedicated group of like-minded friends.

Open your eyes to money, relationships, and abundance by releasing the conscious and unconscious sabotages and blocks to wealth!

Barry Auchettl is one of the world's most successful and qualified vision educators. He has worked with others to improve their vision for over twenty years after founding Eye Power in 1997 and The Vision School in 2018. A fascinating and down-to-earth speaker and facilitator from Australia, he is currently running workshops, speaking engagements, seminars, and trainings worldwide on the topic of increasing one's vibration and stepping into one's life purpose.

www.BarryAuchettl.com

22. DIVINE LEADERSHIP

Christine Kloser

I'll never forget the day. It was December 1, 2010, and the last thread of stability I had was being ripped out from underneath me. As if filing for bankruptcy, losing my home to foreclosure, and having to borrow money to cover basic bills like gas and groceries wasn't bad enough, I was then thrown a curve ball by a former busines partner who wanted to dissolve our partnership and buy my half of the company for a pittance.

The range of emotions I experienced during this time were vast, broad, and deep. Profound sadness, anger, rage, fear, frustration, shock, and hopelessness were among those I felt often. As I rode the waves of emotions and distress, I kept asking myself, "How did I get here?"

I was a smart, motivated, determined woman. I'd been running my own business for nearly twenty years and enjoyed a recognized name and brand, a solid reputation in my industry, hundreds of customers and clients, and work that fulfilled me. How did I end up in the fetal position, crying for hours a day, on the verge of giving up as an entrepreneur, and feeling like a massive failure?

Let me tell you how that happened. But first, let me say that back then I wasn't who I am today, especially regarding how I've grown in my leadership over the past decade. Back then I had been following, to a degree, someone else's idea of what I "should" be doing and who I "should" be. While everyone around me saw me as a strong, effective, and inspiring leader, I felt like I had no idea where I was actually leading myself—or who I was leading myself to be.

I could get 150 people to follow me into a room for one of my live events, but I couldn't lead myself out of a trajectory that didn't feel *right* deep in my soul. Everything looked great on the outside, but inside everything felt wrong. And when you live like that long enough—like I did—the house of cards comes tumbling down and you land in a puddle of tears on the bathroom floor. That was me.

Yet being in that gut-wrenching situation and losing everything (which was especially difficult as the sole income earner in my family) was the exact experience I needed to help me wake up to who I really am and claim my greatness as a Divine Leader.

The interesting thing about losing everything is that it gives you the opportunity to discover that everything you need is within you. I know that sounds trite. I get it. I used to hear that phrase all the time and wonder what it *really* meant. Maybe you've done the same thing too? Or perhaps you're feeling that way right now, thinking, *What the heck do you mean that everything I need is inside me?*

Here's what I mean . . . and this is what Divine Leadership is all about.

What I mean is that whether you are facing a financial challenge, health situation, relationship struggle, career setback, or anything else, *you* are the only one who can actually do anything to change the situation, set a new path, and create more of what you want (and less of what you don't want). But you are not alone in doing that.

When operating under the principles of Divine Leadership, you understand that everything that happens on every level and in every realm and dimension is always unfolding in divine right order. You are loved, supported, and guided every step of the way, and nothing "wrong" can happen . . . ever. Take that in for a moment. Imagine what life could look like when you see every single thing that happens as exactly what's supposed to be happening for *your* highest good, and the highest good of everyone involved. It doesn't matter if you're looking at a personal or family situation, a career or company situation, or a local, national, or global situation. Everything is always happening for your highest healing, growth, and evolution!

Divine Leadership requires this deeper level of proactive, steadfast faith. "Faith in what?" you might ask. Faith that the Universe is a friendly Universe. That life is ever-expanding and evolving in divine right order, all the time. Even when it looks like the opposite of that on the surface.

You see, Divine Leadership isn't about being able to lead others along any particular path. It is about being led by the Divine (through your experiences) into the fullness of who *you* are—into the highest and most magnificent expression of the soul that embodies here and now as you. From that place of inner knowing, you never have to "try" to be a leader. You *are* a leader because of how you show up for yourself, in your life, and in everything you do.

Given the state of our world today and the rapidly evolving times we are living in, it's essential for more and more people to embrace Divine Leadership as a way to live their *own* lives and as a way to show up in the world. Now more than ever, people are hungry for those whose light shines brightly no matter what trouble or chaos may swirl around them. Now more than ever, people want to feel some sense of certainty that they, we, humanity, and the world are going to be OK. And we can't rely on television, magazines, newspapers, or social media to deliver that assuring message. That's why the world needs you to step into your Divine Leadership and be the lighthouse it needs.

For me, stepping into my Divine Leadership was a journey. It took nearly a decade to get from the puddle of tears on the bathroom floor to where I am today. Today, every aspect of my life is working in ways I'd only previously imagined. My business is better than ever. I'm almost fully healed from fifteen years of chronic pain.

My marriage and family are the strongest they've ever been. My desires are being realized with ease, speed, and grace. My creativity is off the charts. And I feel like I am truly living in the f-l-o-w!

Let me share ten key concepts and beliefs that have helped guide me on my path of Divine Leadership. I encourage you to adopt any that resonate with you and embrace them for your journey too.

Ten Key Concepts and Beliefs of Divine Leadership

1. Know you are infinitely loved and supported by life itself.
2. Believe that the Universe is a friendly universe.
3. Embody proactive, steadfast faith.
4. Trust the unfolding process.
5. Have gratitude for what was, what is, and what will be.
6. Believe that your timing is always perfect.
7. Experience deep stillness every day.
8. Know you are exactly where you're meant to be.
9. Envision your deepest desires and feel them already realized and experienced.
10. Understand that you are worthy of receiving and accepting all your desires.

As the subtitle of this book expresses, the journey is about embracing a spiritual path to health, wealth, and love. That said, when you *allow* yourself to be divinely led and *see* yourself as a perfectly designed expression of the Divine, you naturally become the embodiment of Divine Leadership. Through your embodiment, others can't help but experience you as a Divine Leader whose beautiful and powerful presence brings them hope, healing, and a whole new world of possibilities.

When you lead yourself to this place inside of you, and you realize that your presence helps others to access this place of Divine Leadership inside of them, not only does it bring *you* health, wealth, and love, it also makes much more of it possible in the world. And isn't that why you are here? Isn't that why you're reading a book called *Soulful Leadership?* I believe it is. So enjoy the journey of embracing the Divine Leadership that already exists inside of you—embrace being that Divine Leader in the world. We need your light now more than ever. You got this!

Christine Kloser is a *USA Today* and *Wall Street Journal* bestselling author, transformational writing coach, and award-winning publisher. She helps entrepreneurs, leaders, and everyday messengers write and publish transformational books. Since 2007, her programs and services have served 80,000+ authors in more than 100 countries.

www.ChristineKloser.com

Part Three

CONNECTING TO YOUR SOUL TRIBE

As a Soulful Leader, you have the potential to create a powerful ripple of good in the world.

The key to making the impact you are here to make is connecting with your SOUL TRIBE to further expand your **Visibility and Influence.**

Being an entrepreneur is a dynamic expression of Soulful Leadership.

Entrepreneurs have unique opportunities to make a powerful impact in the world while creating personal freedom through self-expression.

As a mission driven entrepreneur, you know that your success depends on reaching your ideal audience with your unique message so you can share your gifts. There are hundreds, maybe even thousands, of people or more, who could benefit from your message or service if they knew what you had to offer.

With the massive growth in the transformation industry and all the shifts that are happening, it can be challenging to cut through the noise and stand out from the crowd. What if it was simple to attract YOUR Soul Tribe of perfect customers, support team, and inspired influencers to promote you?

As the "Great Awakening of Humanity" continues to evolve, we are moving from Fear to Love, Deception to Authenticity, Manipulation to Education, Focus on Money to Focus on Service, Push Marketing to Attraction Marketing, Scarcity Mindset to Abundance Mindset, and from Me to We (from Competition to Collaboration).

You're winning the new game of selling by changing perspectives from the separation thinking of "Me" and "Them" to understanding that "We" are all connected. You're shifting from fear-based marketing focused on pain, lack, and need, to love-based marketing focused on providing desired outcomes, service, and value.

You understand your customers' needs, and you offer solutions that work for them. You no longer need to "push" your products on anyone. Instead you can attract customers to come to you through "Pull" or Attraction Marketing. As an "Evolutionary Entrepreneur," you practice the Art of Soulful Selling through Authenticity, Compassion, Connection, and Results. Soulful Selling is more about how you are "being" than what you are "doing." It starts by aligning with your core values.

As an advocate for those you serve, you understand that the difference between traditional sales and soulful selling is being of service to others rather than just focused on what's in it for you. You listen with your ears, eyes, and heart because you truly connect with your customer. You practice the most important skill in Soulful Selling—cultivating relationships with clients and partners. Going back to the shift from "Me" to "We," you think Win, Win, Win in every situation. If it is not a good deal for everyone, then it's not good for anyone.

Your clients' success stories attract new clients.
People invest in the results you provide.

You are a Pioneer for a new way of being in business.

You are an "Evolutionary Entrepreneur."

23. ATTRACTING YOUR SOUL TRIBE THROUGH ALIGNMENT CONSCIOUSNESS

Mark Porteous

Starting with my birth in the City of Angels, Los Angeles, California, in June of 1970, the Dawn of the Age of Aquarius, "Soulful Leadership" was in my blood and written in the stars. Of course, it's much easier to connect the dots looking backward.

The return home in 1975 to Columbia County, New York, about two and a half hours north of New York City by train, began the third phase of the Hero's Journey for my father. At twenty-three years old, my dad received the call from Spirit to better understand his relationship with God so he could lead others to do the same. He followed his heart west into the sunset with his newlywed sixteen-year-old-bride who would one day be my mom at his side in his brand-new, maroon '64 Mustang convertible to join missionary school.

They returned home from their odyssey ten years later—their minds filled with biblical Scriptures, their hearts filled with love, and their back seat filled with their three children: two daughters (ages seven and two) and one son (age four).

When I was six, my father was a minister at a Dutch Reformed church in the town where both of my parents, my sisters, and I grew up. After my parents divorced, he was banished from the church he had personally built and led. Feeling deeply hurt, he began his personal quest for spiritual truth, and unconsciously, I started my own search for answers.

I would regularly ask my mom questions about spirituality, specifically about Christianity. There seemed to be so much hypocrisy and conflicting messages in the Bible and in the churches I had witnessed. My mom assured me, "I don't know all the answers to your questions, but keep asking and the teachers will come." This book is proof that Mom was right.

My first spiritual teacher came when I was twenty-one, while I was working for Greenpeace International at the Orlando office. My girlfriend brought me to The Spiral Circle bookstore. It was the first time I remember hearing the word *metaphysical*. The bookstore smelled like incense and felt like home.

That's when I read the quote by Pierre Teilhard de Chardin that changed my life forever: "We are not human beings having spiritual experiences. We are spiritual beings having human experiences." Suddenly everything made sense, even beliefs that conflicted with what I had learned from the Bible.

As soon as I got home from the bookstore, I eagerly called my dad, who had written three books by then. I remember anticipating his adoration when I told him I would be following in his footsteps as an author. Instead, his response was, "Don't expect to make money writing a book. You have to have a business, not just a book."

Not one to be easily discouraged, I quickly adjusted my plan to include his advice. I would build a business so I could write for the joy of writing and sharing my beliefs, rather than as a path to wealth. I did not realize at the time that the business could, and perhaps even "should," be related to the book.

I started Unique Ventures, LLC, in 1994 as a vehicle to fund my dream of writing a book.

By 1999 I had over one hundred employees selling souvenirs at amusement parks all over the country. Most of them were teens working summer jobs. One of them was convinced to join my team by her friend, even though she had a full-time job as a medical assistant in a geriatric doctor's office. She was nineteen years old and my most responsible employee. (I would never have guessed that she would become my best friend and that three years later we would be married.)

While I had built a large company, I realized I hadn't written one more word of my book. For the previous five years, it took all I had to run a business that I did not enjoy so that I could pursue my passion, which I had no time to even explore, much less pursue.

So I sold my business and got a job in sales. I figured I could make more money in less time and finally have time to finish my book. In my mind, I would have the book done within two years, and then I could decide what to do with the rest of my life.

After many years of putting off my passion and purpose in exchange for the "golden handcuffs" of a safe yet soul-crushing corporate sales job, everything changed in April 2010 when our twins were born. I still had not made any progress with my book. Instead, I had gotten comfortable in a job that provided a great income and benefits.

While the previous ten years seemed like a blur, with newborn twins, I knew the next ten years would go by even faster. A terrible fear came over me. I was very clear that if I did not make a change, I would be teaching my children the deferred lifestyle of putting off their dreams to live up to someone else's expectations or pursue what society suggested as the safe and responsible path. I did not want to teach my children to give up on their dreams.

When Renée was six months pregnant with Eden and Xen, she surprised me with tickets to Dr. Wayne Dyer's limited theatrical release of *Wishes Fulfilled*. He described a shift in human consciousness that was happening. He explained that we were approaching a critical mass of just one percent of the human population raising their consciousness, which would become the tipping point of a quantum leap into the next evolution of collective human consciousness. My whole body lit up, and I knew with absolute clarity that I was here to share my gifts for the shift.

By the time our twins had their first birthday, my first book, *The Human Experience*, was written and, with Renée's help, I self-published it through Amazon. Just after my forty-first birthday, we celebrated with a book launch at a favorite local cafe with seventy-plus of my closest friends.

Then my wife asked, "Now what? You've been wanting to write this book for eighteen years. What do you want to do now?"

I had no answer. She suggested life coaching. Honestly, I didn't know much about it. In fact, I considered life coaching to be a new form of therapy for wealthy housewives. Little did I know it was a huge and growing industry.

The first thing we did was research to find out how much money I could make. With a quick Google search, we learned the average life coach was making under $20,000 per year. After ten years of making over $100,000 per year on average, $20K was not going to provide a lifestyle we would enjoy.

Then Renée asked me a profound question. She said, "That's what the *average* life coach makes. You've never been an average sales rep, so why do you think you would be an average life coach?"

So then we looked into what the top coaches were making. People like Tony Robbins were making millions, while many others were making over $100,000 per year. I figured if they could do it, I could too. As I researched, I found plenty of people promising that if I did exactly what they did, I too could be quickly making $10,000 per month with ease.

I decided to test it out by enrolling in a coaching certification program. My coach asked me what my niche was going to be. Although I was not familiar with niching, I said I wanted to be a spiritual coach. He literally laughed at me and said, "You won't make any money as a spiritual coach. You need to choose Health, Wealth, or Love, and you can sneak in spirituality like medicine in the dog food."

I bought that lie for my first five years as a business coach and JV strategist. I tried to conform to what I thought was expected of me. Even while investing thousands of dollars doing deep spiritual work and supporting clients who were highly successful spiritual coaches, subconsciously I continued to believe the lie. Now, however, I am clear that for me there is no other choice than Leading with Soul—and the rest will follow.

Five years after making the leap from the corporate ladder to follow my purpose and passion, I was struggling to generate the revenue I needed to provide for my family. I had invested tens of thousands of dollars. All the business blueprints that I tried failed to produce the BIG results they promised. I wondered how I could guide others to thrive in their purpose if I was not thriving in mine. Desperate for hope, my wife begged me to consider going back to my corporate job.

I was painfully torn between continuing to follow my inner guidance to live my mission and my ego mind that feared I might not be able to take care of my family's basic needs.

I even started to question my stand. Did I really believe that every human challenge has a spiritual solution, especially in my business? And, if so, where should I look for those solutions?

That's when I began experimenting with something I call "Alignment Consciousness" as a practice to discover for myself if spiritual fulfillment could make a positive impact in my business by trusting my inner guidance for all choices, both personal and professional.

Everything is spiritual, even Sales and Marketing.

Once I decided to lead with soul, my life completely changed for the better.

While reading *The Untethered Soul* by Michael Singer, I made the decision to follow my inner guidance as my primary compass, no matter what. Suddenly everything began to shift. Synchronicities led to opportunities I could have never expected. I began to experience great joy and ease in my work. Clients seemed to be magnetized to me.

I was beginning to live my stand. The more I was true to who I am, the more magical my life became.

Over the last ten years, I've helped soulful leaders grow their audience, transform thousands of lives, and generate hundreds of thousands of dollars in additional revenue. In 2020, while businesses around the world struggled and many closed their doors, the twenty members of my MetaMind and I were having our best year ever.

In high school my friends called me Mark Party-us. Now my friends call me Mark Partner-us. Ultimately, I see my role as hosting a Soul Family Reunion to support the Great Awakening of Human Consciousness.

Who do you get to BE to attract your Soul Tribe?

Mark Porteous, "The Soul Connector," is a husband, the father of twins, a Joint Venture Strategist, an Affiliate Concierge, and the co-founder of the Soul Affiliate Alliance. Transformational Leaders hire Mark to reach more people with their message by developing soulful alliances so they can make a greater impact in the world while enjoying more freedom and ease.

www.MarkPorteous.com

24. RELATIONSHIP CAPITAL: THE MOST IMPORTANT CURRENCY FOR SOULFUL LEADERSHIP

Debra Poneman

My son Daniel has always loved basketball. As soon as he could walk without holding on, his favorite activity was putting his little plastic basketball in the bright blue and yellow Fisher-Price hoop.

For his fifth birthday, while all the other kids had their birthday bashes in their backyards or basements (or if they were lucky, at the perennial favorite, Chuck E. Cheese), Daniel insisted that his celebration of the big five be held at Michael Jordan's restaurant. The highlight moment was when he had his picture taken next to the showcase housing Michael Jordan's shoe.

When he was a freshman in high school, he made the A-team, but since this white boy decidedly could not jump, he spent pretty much the entire season warming the bench. Yet his place on the A-team was not for naught. As he traveled with the team all season, he developed an eye for talent. He could look at a player and tell if he was material to be recruited by a Division I school. He could even predict who might have what it takes to make it into the NBA one day.

Daniel, ever the entrepreneur, decided to start a basketball scouting website at the ripe old age of fifteen. He would take video footage of Chicago-area high school players and post them on his website along with his evaluation of the player.

As news of his exceptional scouting abilities spread, he soon became known as the go-to scout in Chicago for college coaches around the country looking for high school talent. In fact, he became so well known that ABC, CNN, Comcast Sports, the *New York Times*, the *Chicago Tribune*, and numerous other media outlets did features on the "Boy Scout." There was even a full-page feature article about him in *Sports Illustrated* titled, "Why College Hoops Coaches Seek the Advice of a Sixteen-Year-Old Scout."

One day Daniel realized that the players who might be recruited by Division I schools were getting a lot of exposure, but the only way the potential Division II and III kids were being seen was if they paid to be in showcases which were put on as for-profit events. The hefty price tag to be in these events was often out of reach for the players, so Daniel decided to put on his own showcase. The cost was seventy-five dollars per player. This didn't seem like a huge price for the potential to be seen by a college coach and hopefully be offered a life-changing scholarship. But Daniel soon discovered that most of the potential showcase participants didn't have the seventy-five dollars or, in many cases, the money for transportation to get to the showcase. Eventually Daniel scrapped the fee and lost thousands.

And that was the catalyst for the formation of Daniel's nonprofit, Shot in the Dark Foundation. The plan was to solicit donations from philanthropic-minded folks so the players could play for free and have a chance to get a scholarship and an opportunity for a radically different life.

Daniel's first showcase had about thirty college coaches and one hundred players. His last one had 130 college coaches and 360 players. To date, his foundation has generated close to 50 million dollars in college scholarships.

So, you ask, what does this have to do with soulful leadership or relationship capital?

One day, after a very successful showcase that was clearly going to generate millions in scholarship dollars for the kids in attendance, I asked Daniel, who up to this point had not taken a penny for himself, if there was a way that he could maybe make some money.

"Mom, just be patient," he replied. "I'm building relationship capital."

That sounded like a good idea, so I let go . . . for a while.

As time went on, I watched as he helped player after player get lucrative scholarships through his showcases, as well as from the individual highlight videos he sent out. After a while it again became difficult for me to be patient. I loved what he was doing and was immensely proud of him, but given the long hours he spent day in and day out, I once more had to broach the subject.

"There must be some way for you to make money for yourself in this endeavor," I ventured.

His reply was a more emphatic, "Mom, you'll see, when I do this for no reason other than that I want to see these players succeed, just trust me that I'll end up getting more back than money. Just hang in there."

And hang in there I did. Within a short time, NBA players looking for a way to give back to their communities began supporting Daniel's showcases, with the NBA itself giving matching funds. Shoe companies with household names became sponsors. And when Daniel decided to make a documentary on high school basketball in the inner city, someone with whom Daniel had built relationship capital invested hundreds of thousands of dollars to cover the cost of production. The film was bought by FOX and nominated for an Emmy.

And the story continues. Daniel's nonprofit, now managed by a team of devoted Chicagoans, left Daniel free to start his own sports management firm, one that's now recognized as "a firm to watch" in the competitive arena of athlete management. The investor in his new firm was—you guessed it—someone with whom Daniel had built relationship capital.

One day, as I was marveling on how vast his influence had become in the world of sports, I complimented him and said, "Thank you, Daniel, for teaching me about relationship capital. You were absolutely right. Building it really paid off in the end. It's a brilliant concept."

His reply both surprised me and touched my heart, as he said, "Why are you thanking me, Mom? I learned it from you. You teach in your seminars that you need to treat everyone as the most important person in the world. You always say that the person standing in front of you at any given moment deserves your full attention and not to judge. You tell your students that no matter that person's age or ethnicity or station in life, they deserve your respect simply because they're a human being—and I see how you actually do that with everyone. I just gave the concept a name. I did what I did because I loved doing it, but you also taught me the law of karma. And look how relationship capital has played out in your life!"

I thanked him for the reminder—and he was right.

When I started my Yes to Success company in the early 1980s, a beautiful young college student approached me and asked if she could work for my company. I gave her my full attention and listened intently to all of her ideas without looking around the room to see if there was somebody else more important I should be talking to.

She became my secretary/assistant, and when I came down with the flu and couldn't fly to New York to give a seminar, she went for me. That was her first speaking engagement. That young woman, Marci Shimoff, is now one of the most successful speakers in the US and, as the women's face of the Chicken Soup for the Soul franchise, has sold over 16 million *Chicken Soup* books as well as her own *New York Times* bestsellers *Happy for No Reason* and *Love for No Reason*.

When Marci had the idea for *Chicken Soup for the* American Idol *Soul* and then couldn't write it since she was under contract for *Happy for No Reason*, to whom do you think she handed a lay-down bestseller? Let's just say it was someone who had quite the account filled with relationship capital.

When *New York Times* bestselling author Janet Attwood was virtually homeless, living on a couch at a meditation center and jumping over a fence to take showers in the next-door neighbor's pool house, someone gave her the money to attend my Yes to Success seminar. It impacted her life so profoundly that she, too, asked if she could work for me. She also became one of my "secretaries" (as we called them at the time!), and eventually I had her teach part of my seminar, and then another part, and then another. She, too, now travels the world teaching others how to live their passion to sell-out crowds in Japan, China, Thailand, Norway, Denmark, and more.

And when my kids were grown and I was ready to go back on the speaking circuit after a twenty-one-year hiatus of being a stay-at-home mom, who do you think secured for me my first speaking engagement . . . and my second . . . and my third, until I was firmly back in the saddle? Yes, it was Janet, someone with whom I had an account full of relationship capital.

Soulful leadership is about looking for opportunities to help people become the greatest versions of themselves. It's about deeply caring about the people who look up to us. It's about finding ways to uplift those who have put their trust in us. It's not about how *I* can win, but how *we* can win.

We are in the middle of a revolution. It's a soulful revolution, and we are the leaders of this revolution. We are the ones who will bring the aspect of the soul into the areas of business and politics and into our schools and all of our institutions. It's a revolution that will lead us into a future where problems will be solved by our hearts overruling our minds, where kindness will trump cunning, and cooperation will change the face of competition.

It's a revolution where people will enter not only personal interactions, but also business transactions, not with the thought, *What's in it for me?* but rather, *What's in it for us? What can I give? How can I serve? How can I win without anyone else losing?*

The leaders of this revolution will rely more on intuition, and the more we listen to our intuition, the better it will serve us.

The leaders of this revolution will need to lead by example. If you're telling your people to be one way or do one thing and you're being and doing another, you may have been able to get away with it a few years ago, but no more. In 2020 people have vision like never before. They're like your children—they have your number. They see exactly what's going on. You can't get away with anything.

This soulful revolution is about heart connection. The expression, "People don't care what you know until they know that you care," has never been as true as it is today.

This revolution is about never forgetting the sacredness of *every* human being because we are all created in the image and likeness of God. As Mahatma Gandhi so powerfully taught us: "If you cannot see God in the next person you meet, you need look no further."

The respect with which we treat the founder of our company is the same respect we need to show the young man who takes our order at Burger King. The deference we show those we hold in esteem, such as our religious and spiritual leaders, is the same deference we need to show our neighbors down the street, even when their car alarm keeps going off. The kindness we extend to our favored child is the same kindness we need to extend to the homeless man panhandling at the stoplight.

That's how you build relationship capital—and that's how you live as a soulful leader.

Debra Poneman, bestselling author and founder of Yes to Success Seminars, has created a system, now used by tens of thousands of people around the world, to create lives of not only success and abundance, but of deep happiness, self-love, lasting inner fulfillment, and contribution to a world that works for everyone.

https://yestosuccess.com/

25. THE MAGIC OF SACRED SYNCHRONICITY

Jan H. Stringer

It all started as a sales and marketing strategy consisting of five seemingly simple steps. They were designed to help business owners stop the struggle and confusion about finding customers and shift their perspective to attract them.

Each time I worked with an individual or a group, there was a sigh of relief when people discovered that sales and marketing could be much easier than they had thought, and many of their fears about their businesses melted away. Many people think that they are not good at sales or marketing; however, when I share my definition of sales and marketing as "building relationship" and share my strategy, they have an immediate increase in their confidence and their sales results.

These are the five steps:

- The first inquiry gives focus and clarity: Describe the qualities, characteristics, and attributes of your perfect customer/client.
- The second is a deep dive about the relationship: Identify what makes you and your perfect customer/client tick.
- The third is about what is perfect for you: Specify what you want your perfect customer/client to expect of you.
- The fourth creates how you want to be seen in the world: Declare who I am BEE-ing.

The fifth kicks things off: Take attractive actions.

Together these five steps are called **Strategic Attraction™ Planning**, and in the process of going through this simple process, people gain clarity and focus about who they want to be working with, and when they become clear, the people they are meant to be serving are irresistibly drawn to them.

The fun part in all of this is how people seem to "find" you through the most magical ways. Many times, when these connections start to happen, you might describe it as something that came to you "out-of-the-blue" or as "kismet" or "serendipity." I call it *Strategic Synchronicity™*: the out-of-the-blue connections that come to you after completing the Strategic Attraction™ Planning process.

What has become clear for me after working with tens of thousands of people around the globe is that there is another stratum beyond Strategic Attraction™ Planning that I call the **Magic of SACRED SYNCHRONICITY**.

Over the years that you are in business, of all the relationships that will come and go, some will become much more than your perfect customers. These are your golden friends. These are the sacred ones, your *Anam Caras*, your Soul Friends.

You know who these people are because they stick with you beyond business. They spend time with you, they revere you, you feel warm and special with them, and the relationship is expansive. These friends share about you with others from the highest place of love and respect.

And when you meet them for the first time, there is a soul recognition, whether or not you know it at the time.

These sacred friendships impact the rest of your life, and together you will impact the world. They are spiritual relationships that take you closer to God and help you to see who you are at a soul level.

Sacred Synchronicity happens when your deepest inner values and core purpose align inwardly. It happens when you go beyond the basic level of Strategic Attraction™ Planning and step into your true purpose or calling in every interaction with the people you meet and hang out with.

From this inner alignment, you begin to operate at a higher vibration that goes beyond the strategy. And it is no longer a business strategy—it is a way of life. Many times it comes like an answer to your prayers and turns out better than what you had imagined was possible. That is the Magic of Sacred Synchronicity.

Let me leave you with a few personal examples of the Magic of Sacred Synchronicity that have happened over the last twenty years in my own business.

In 2001 my first book, *Attracting Perfect Customers: The Power of Strategic Synchronicity*, had just been released. I was attending a NIA Dance class, something I loved so much that I enjoyed dancing at a particular studio in Houston, Texas, three times a week or more. There I met a tall man named Alan Davidson. We both loved NIA and shared this common joy of movement. One day he asked me about my new book, and that was the beginning of a sacred connection that has been completely synchronistic. Something was sparked in our common love for dance that drew our soul imprints together. Over time it became clear that this was so much more than just a friendship; it developed into a soul alliance. Alan became an ambassador for my work, and he helped birth the idea of Sacred Synchronicity by reflecting my soul's purpose to me in a special VIP Session.

Alan Hickman called me after hearing about my book and training from a friend of his in Fairfield, Iowa. He said that when he thumbed through the book, his first thought was that "these ladies are doing what I have wanted to do my whole life." This Sacred Connection began when he had that thought, and it continued when he came to my training in Houston. Little did Alan and I know that the serendipity that brought us together would result in thirteen years as business and marriage partners until his death in 2017. We were united in our sacred purpose, and I chose Alan to be my life partner because I saw that our soul visions were meant to be expressed together through our business to the world. When he came to Houston to attend the training, my heart and soul took a leap of faith as I realized that he was my sacred life partner, the one that I had been praying for, and here he was standing right beside me, ready to play in this journey together.

While attending a Joint Venture marketing conference, I was sitting near one of my new friends that I had met at the same conference the year before. He introduced me to his conference roommate, Mark Porteous. I remember that I felt honored to meet him because he knew everyone at that conference, and I marveled at his wide network of connections. Little did I know that he and I would cross paths many times over the next few years. He attended my certification training program, where I became more acquainted with his amazing, soulful resonance. Our connection grew, and as I started to consider my twenty-year departure from teaching Strategic Attraction™ Planning, the only person who showed up as a possible person to carry on my legacy was Mark.

Julia Stege showed up at a retreat that I was leading in Houston at a wonderful place called White Eagle Lodge. She had been participating in the SACAT (Strategic Attraction Certification and Training), and this event was part of the program. After a magical retreat, Julia became a loyal, raving fan from her experience there. She is a perfect example of how relationships grow beyond business. We have become soul friends over the years. Julia and I both share our common love of Strategic Attraction, and she has become well known for it with her own clientele. I count our friendship as a Sacred Synchronicity because we could have never predicted that our friendship would last for fifteen years—and I imagine it will continue for a long time to come.

You might be wondering, "How can I make Sacred Synchronicity happen?"

Since the magic of Sacred Synchronicity is in how it shows up in the most unexpected ways, there is no special strategy or plan to make it happen. However, when you align your soul with your destiny, more occasions of synchronicity will show up for you. Learn to become more awake and aware each moment.

Whenever you meet someone, notice whether that person resonates with your soul, and then be prepared for the magic to start working for you. I look forward to hearing about your experiences of magical connections and the fun of having sacred soul friends in your business and life.

Jan H. Stringer, founder of Perfect Customers, Inc., is the author of two bestsellers, *Attracting Perfect Customers: The Power of Strategic Synchronicity* and *BEE-ing Attraction: What Love Has to Do with Business and Marketing*. A popular speaker and coach, she is the creator of the Strategic Attraction™ STARS Certification Program for coaches, trainers, and speakers.

www.PerfectCustomers.com

26. MY ACCIDENTAL TRIBE

David Riklan

When I began my career after college, the furthest idea from my mind was creating a tribe of thirty-five thousand experts—all sharing the same mission of improving people's lives. Fast-forward several decades later: I am running Self-Growth.com, a very popular self-improvement website with over 35,793 experts providing articles, products, and events to millions of visitors every year.

My accidental tribe-building story begins with my first serious job after college. Shortly after graduating from the University of Buffalo with a Chemical Engineering degree, I went to work for Hewlett-Packard as a sales representative.

As much as I had a penchant for science and engineering, I also enjoyed socializing and interacting with people. Sitting behind a desk working on Chemical Engineering problems was not the future that I had envisioned. The Hewlett-Packard sales position provided me with a very unique situation: selling computer solutions to engineers and scientists. I would be able to leverage my technical knowledge and interact with people on a daily basis. Where better to combine my two strengths than to work for one of the top-ranked companies in the world?

One interesting facet about my job at HP is the company's commitment to excellence and the closely aligned commitment to training their employees to be as effective as possible. They demonstrated these commitments by providing a wide range of internal training programs while still allowing me ample opportunity to pursue training outside of the company. They wanted to build their sales team into the most effective sales team in the industry.

With the Hewlett Packard training, I took the opportunity to supplement their internal training by taking a course one evening a week from Dale Carnegie called "Effective Speaking in Human Relations." One evening a week didn't seem too overwhelming.

Prior to taking the course, I didn't know a lot about Dale Carnegie or the personal development industry. The course was designed to teach people to communicate more effectively, both in one-on-one situations and in public speaking settings. It seemed like a great fit for my current career trajectory.

The course helped me develop my communications skills, but it was a specific student in the class that made a lasting impact on me.

When I entered the class on the first day, I noticed a disheveled woman dressed in tattered clothes hovering in the corner of the room. I thought she was part of the cleaning staff. It turned out that she was one of the approximately forty students taking the class. She was shy, not particularly well-spoken, and extremely uncomfortable introducing herself and speaking in front of the class.

Over the course of the next fourteen weeks, however, I watched this woman go from appearing to be part of the cleaning service to running for office in the New York City political system. I watched this woman's transformation with both awe and yearning.

Over that same time period, I continued to develop my speaking and listening skills. By the end of the fourteen-week program, I knew in my heart that something special had occurred—and I needed to be part of it. I contacted the instructor and explained that I loved what they were doing and wanted to be more involved.

They offered me the opportunity to take the course again for free as a Graduate Assistant (GA). My job would be to assist the instructor from the back of the room and demonstrate the individual talks. I was all in.

This moment in time was a major shifting point for me, moving my life trajectory into a completely different direction. Up until I took this course, I firmly believed that learning was for school and college. After graduation, the focus would be on one's career and job. I was aware of the importance of job training, but I thought that my personal development was complete.

The Dale Carnegie training opened my eyes to the fact that learning, changing, and transforming can be a lifelong adventure. I just loved that concept.

Becoming a Graduate Assistant was so impactful that I wanted more. I became a GA a second time around, but I still wanted more. I wanted to be an instructor.

The natural question came up: "What is involved with being an instructor?"

It was simple, but not easy. I would need to go through their advanced training and work with another instructor to demonstrate my ability. I decided it was well worth the investment.

Months later, I was an official Dale Carnegie instructor working part-time one evening a week. I was living parallel lives—my life at Hewlett-Packard and my career in computers during the day and my commitment to Dale Carnegie and personal development in the evening.

My interest in personal development continued to grow, and I went on to take courses and learn from Zig Ziglar, Brian Tracy, and Tony Robbins. I invested in courses from Nightingale Conant, and I started consuming a lot of this material.

In the back of my head, an idea started to blossom. Corporate America was good and had its perks, but I had a new dream growing in my mind. I wanted to have my own business, and it was going to be some sort of self-improvement business.

I wasn't sure what it was or how it was going to work, but one day, somehow, it would become a reality. I wanted to have an impact; I wanted to change people's lives. I wanted to continue improving my life, and I wanted to help other people improve their lives.

I continued with Hewlett-Packard and eventually explored several different areas of interest. My primary career focus continued to be sales and marketing in the area of technology. I worked in scientific visualization, organic chemistry databases, and process engineering, While I was jumping back and forth between sales and marketing for a range of companies, I never left my dream of creating my own self-improvement company. Over the years, I continued to take courses on the side.

Fast-forward to 1995. The internet had started becoming more popular, and it became clear to me that the internet was going to change literally everything. I was still working in Corporate America, but I decided to try something on the side. I wasn't ready to quit my job, yet I still had my passion for self-improvement,

I remember thinking, *This is crazy, but run with this. You've wanted to run with this your whole life.* On November 13, 1995, I bought the domain name selfgrowth.com.

I didn't know how to make a website myself, so I hired one of the top experts of the day to help me: a high school kid. And this high school kid knew more about websites than most people. I started building this website with a very simple mission: I wanted to aggregate information about different websites that had to do with the self-improvement industry.

Over the course of my career in sales and marketing, it became clear to me that there were a lot of programs out there. Whether you wanted to improve your health, your finances, relationships, your spirituality, or your mental health, there were many programs to choose from. If you want to lose weight or learn to set goals, you could find a program to teach you what you needed to know. No one program would work for everybody. There was no panacea, no cure-all, so I wanted to bring together information about all the top websites and programs.

I created a Yahoo-type directory for self-improvement. If someone needed help with goal setting, they could find multiple goal-setting websites. If they needed help with time management, they could find time-management websites.

All I really did was identify the best resources, and people started coming to the website. I started building up traffic. As I was sitting there waiting for people to come to my website, I started to think that there had to be a better way; there had to be some way to proactively control it.

It was time to create my own email newsletter. I put up a link on selfgrowth.com that invited people to sign up for my free newsletter. People would provide me with their name and email address, and I would regularly email them information. Back in the 1990s, this was still a revolutionary idea.

Within hours of the new link going up, people started subscribing. Every week I diligently wrote a newsletter. My dad, a psychologist, started writing content for my newsletter as well. I quickly realized that writing all the content on my own was going to be tedious and time-consuming and wouldn't get me where I wanted to go.

I made a decision. I needed to start reaching out to other people; I needed to develop a community of people who could provide me with content. I didn't use the word *tribe* at the time, but that's what I essentially told myself when I wanted to build a supportive community.

The day I reached out to my first author to use their content, I accidentally started building my tribe. I began finding experts with great content, and I solicited their support for publishing their information on selfgrowth.com. I published their information in my newsletters as well as directly on my website.

I collected content on goal setting and stress management and health and relationships. Unbeknownst to me, I was building a community of my own—a tribe of people out there who were helping me build selfgrowth.com.

The results were amazing: the more content I had on the website, the more traffic I generated, and the more people were reading the content. The experts that had become part of my community helped me build and attract even more people. Soon I had a directory of websites and a directory of articles. The compensation for all these experts was free visibility to their business. It was a very symbiotic relationship.

In order to enhance the community, I created expert pages or profiles. The concept was very simple. I gave all the experts an opportunity to create profiles for themselves, highlighting their expertise—more free exposure. Ten expert profiles turned into one hundred, then one thousand, and then five thousand. Today selfgrowth.com has become a community of over thirty-five thousand experts, all providing content, articles, websites, and blogs.

The accidental need for more content drove me to build this community, and this community has enabled selfgrowth.com to become one of the top self-improvement websites in the world.

Several years ago, using Google Analytics, I did an analysis of our overall website traffic and found that more than 100 million unique visitors have come to selfgrowth.com. Selfgrowth.com has literally impacted 100 million unique people from over 126 different countries. And this all happened because I accidentally built a tribe.

After I began creating my first tribe, I quickly realized that a team or a tribe can always help expand one's mission exponentially. We don't have to take this journey alone. Isn't it time to accidentally build your own tribe?

David Riklan is founder of SelfGrowth.com, one of the top self-improvement and personal growth websites. SelfGrowth.com gets millions of visitors a year. His company also publishes two email newsletters going out to over 275,000 weekly subscribers on the topics of self-improvement, natural health, and personal growth.

www.SelfGrowth.com

27. YOUR CLIENT'S TRANSFORMATIONAL JOURNEY

Alan Davidson

Can the art of great storytelling be your key to more sales, more money, and the ultimate success of your business? When you tell your client's story well, you betcha!

Crafting your **Client's Transformational Journey** and telling it well can be a game changer for your success and your bottom line. This applies no matter what business you are in as a Soulful Entrepreneur: healer, therapist, bodyworker, author, coach, or creative. It applies whether you are just starting out or quite experienced with a six- or seven-figure business.

The age-old adage in sales is "A confused mind does not buy." If you tell a muddled and confusing story to your Divine Audience (my fave way of saying "perfect clients"):

1. They can't see the vision of what's possible for them and their life.
2. They will not see how your unique, signature transformation can truly help them.
3. They simply will not buy from you.

If your Divine Audience chooses not to invest in their transformation with you, then the impact you are destined to make in this world slips away. When you tell your **Client's Transformational Journey** fabulously, your message will be clear, concise, and relatable.

Everything you need to grow your business and speak to your perfect customers is in the **Client's Transformational Journey**. Your **Client's Transformational Journey** requires time to craft, but when you do, you can hone the story to create a sixty-second elevator speech, a two- to three-minute introduction, a signature speech, or your sales webinar. Your message will magnetize those who resonate with it, and that leads to sales.

So let me tell you a story . . .

Stories are the single common denominator that connects us to each other, heart-to-heart. As humans, we have communicated through stories for thousands of years: from ancient campfires, stone amphitheaters, and reading a book to today's IMAX movies, HD TV, and podcasts.

I have been fascinated by storytelling since 1978 when I took my first advanced psychology class. I've been a student of human nature ever since, wondering what it means to be human, the mental and spiritual building blocks of our personalities, sociology, philosophy, religion, the psychology of sales, and so on.

My influences for crafting this **Client's Transformation Journey** are:

- Carl G. Jung, one of the grandfathers of psychiatry. He has been the greatest influence, especially with his definitions of archetypes. I consider myself a Carl Jung fanboy.
- Joseph Campbell's work with the "Hero's Journey" obviously has had a great impact on my work.
- Michael Hauge is a Hollywood script writer and the author of *The Hero's 2 Journeys*. His insights into the hero's internal and external transformation are brilliant.

- Jeff Walker, my marketing mentor, is the creator of the online Product Launch Formula, and always says every product launch is a good story told well.
- Don Miller, the creator of Story Brand has also shaped my thinking by simplifying the steps of the "Hero's Journey."

I stand on the shoulders of each of these great storytellers. After eleven years as a Product Launch Strategist, and more than 125 product launches and marketing campaigns, I know that storytelling is not only a good idea or a great theory, but it really works in the real world. Your **Client's Transformational Journey** helps you make sales, change lives, and have a greater impact in our world.

The Eight Steps of Your Client's Transformational Story

Let me share the same story crafting process I take every one of my VIP Product Launch Strategy clients through. During this $20K, two-day VIP Intensive, we laser-focus the first day on crafting **the product creators' Client's Transformational Journey**. Getting this story right is the secret sauce for every successful launch and marketing campaign I've designed.

This story, told well, works in real-life marketing campaigns—using elements for the very first email through all the launch content, or free video series; the sales webinar; the cart open to the cart close; all the way through to the product delivery. Collectively these stories and experiences create the transformation you've promised your Divine Audience.

But first, I'll share the eight steps I work through by applying them to the story of Neo in the movie *The Matrix*:

1. The Client's Future Self – "The One" is what Morpheus calls the hero who is destined to end the war between Humanity and the Machines, the creators of the Matrix.

2. The Client – Thomas A. Anderson is a man living two lives. By day he is an average computer programmer; by night he is a hacker known as Neo.

3. Has a Problem – Neo spends untold hours creating software hacks and seeking the answer to a very important question: "What is the Matrix?" That is his internal problem. Neo also has an external problem. Agent Smith has come to arrest him so he can trap the elusive Morpheus.

4. Meets a Guide – Morpheus is commander of the rebel ship, the *Nebuchadnezzar*. Morpheus fearlessly leads his team to liberate the bodies of the hackers who are ready to realize the truth of the Matrix. Inside the Matrix, he is the most-wanted criminal hacker. The Agents will go to any lengths to arrest and kill Morpheus.

5. The Guide Gives Him a Plan – Morpheus, Neo's new Guide, offers him a plan. The Plan starts with two options . . .

- Take the Blue Pill, and Neo will return to his drab world, back in his bed, continuing to live in ignorance and illusion, forgetting that any of this happened.
- Take the Red Pill and dive down a rabbit hole of truth—and find the answer to his question, "What is the Matrix?"

Neo accepts Morpheus' plan and takes the Red Pill.

6. And Calls Him to Action – Now comes Morpheus' first call to action: Neo must up-level his combat skills and begin his training as The One.

There's a wonderful scene where Neo wakes up from a ten-hour programming download and says, "I know Kung Fu."

Morpheus replies, "Show me."

In a fabulous Kung Fu match, Morpheus and Neo spar fist-to-fist, kick-to-kick, mind-to-mind.

Neo is on the path to becoming The One with many more calls to action: The Jump Program, The Oracle, and Dueling with Agent Smith.

7. **What Happens if He Fails?** – What's at risk if Neo fails at becoming The One? If he dies inside the Matrix, he dies in the real world. And if Neo dies, then Humanity will never be free of the Matrix and will live in slavery for eternity.

8. **What Happens When He Succeeds?** – By the end of the movie, Neo fights a brutal battle against several vicious Agents. Neo realizes that he is The One and that he can bend and transcend the rules of the Matrix. Morpheus laid out the plan for him to succeed . . . and introduced him to his Future Self: The One who could win the war for all humanity against The Machines. Neo, Morpheus, and Humanity have at least won the first battle.

Your Client's Transformational Journey

1. **Your Client's Future Self** – Who will they be after working with you over the course of their investment, whether that is ninety days, six months, or a year? What are the new skills they will have? What does their life look like after solving their most painful and expensive problem? How do they, and their friends, describe them now?

2. **The Client** – At soul level you incarnated with a Soul Purpose and a Soul Destiny, complete with a Divine Audience to serve. These are the people you are destined to touch, work with, and help to transform their lives.

People want success at a higher level, but in general, they are unskilled. There is a gap between what they want and the skills they need to get their transformation.

What are the qualities, characteristics, and attributes of your Divine Audience?

3. **The Client Has a Problem** – Your Client thinks they have one problem, but they actually have three problems: an External problem, an Internal problem, and a Universal problem.

The five External Problems in which people will make a significant investment are:

- Health and Wellness
- Relationships and Conflict

- Making Money with Meaning and Purpose
- Peak Performance or Leadership
- Spiritual Connection or Soul Purpose

A lot of coaches and healers make the mistake of focusing only on external problems, on the symptom and not the cause, so solutions don't stick permanently.

What is the painful External Problem your Divine Audience needs to solve?

What is the Internal Problem they need to solve to get the external success they say they want (usually some variation of fear and self-doubt)?

The Universal Problem is the ultimate realization of the Soul having a Human experience with the embodiment of Peace, Love, or Joy. The spiritual values that drive our very human choices are the bridges we can use to realize the Soul's Purpose.

To be effective and get results for your client, you have to help them solve the External and Internal problems, or at least take the first major steps to solving them. You're golden when you solve all three problems: Internal, External, and Universal.

1. **The Client Meets a Guide** – Every Hero needs a guide: Frodo has Gandalf; Luke Skywalker has Obi-Wan Kenobi; Harry Potter has Dumbledore; and Katniss Everdeen has Haymitch.

As the Guide, your client sees you as the expert. When you step into your own fabulousness as a Guide, you then deliver the transformation that only you can to your Divine Audience.

Every successful Guide requires three essential qualities: Expertise, Empathy, and Engagement.

Your Divine Audience needs to know that you have *expertise* and authority, that you've helped yourself and/or others with similar problems, that you get real results in the real world. Your expertise gives them confidence that they can develop the new skills they need to succeed.

Empathy lets your client know that you feel their pain, that you have their back, and that you will firmly guide them to solve the external, internal, and universal problems that hamper their progress.

Engagement helps you keep your Divine Audience's interest over the long-term. You must share your success stories, as well as your own experiences, to keep people connected to you. The more authentic and unique you are, the more you will lead, inspire, and impact your Divine Audience.

2. **The Guide Gives the Client a Plan** – Create a three-, five-, or seven-step Success Path. Your plan is the simple-to-understand strategy your clients will follow to get the transformation they say they want and that you will deliver.

3. **You Call the Client to Action** – You invite them to undertake the transformational journey by saying "Yes!" emotionally, physically, spiritually, and financially. Hiring you as the Guide is when they answer the call. You will hold them accountable to take new actions and to make progress possible.

4. **What Happens if They Fail?** – What is the high cost of staying stuck in the status quo, of failing to learn new skills, knowledge, and expanding their competencies? What is the high price of stewing in self-doubt, fear, and insecurity? You must remind them of the high price of failing to change.

5. **What Happens When They Succeed?** – What will their life be like when they succeed? They know in their heart of hearts that there is a Vision of their life fulfilled, happy, healthy, or financially free. Listen deeply to their Vision of their successful life . . . and paint a vivid picture of that Vision.

What do Homer's *Odyssey* and Dante's *Divine Comedy* have in common with Tolkien's *The Lord of the Rings* and Steven Spielberg's *Raiders of the Lost Ark?* They are all stories about a hero on a quest, searching for a fabulous treasure, or a more mysterious priceless object such as the Holy Grail.

Your Divine Audience is on its own unique quest—to defeat the powers of "playing small, being the best-kept secret, and being broke."

It is up to you to tell THEIR story—and tell it well. Crafting your **Client's Transformational Journey** is also the best gift you can give to your Divine Audience, your business, and yourself.

Alan Davidson is the midwife of Evolutionary Mystic Meditation and founder of www.ThroughYourBody.com. He was named the 2007 Glazer-Kennedy Inner Circle Houston Marketer-of-the-Year for his savvy business and marketing skills. Alan completed Jeff Walker's Product Launch Manager training in 2009. He helps body-mind-spirit entrepreneurs launch their products and services.

www.ThroughYourBody.com

28. "MORE, PLEASE"—SELLING WITH LOVE

Sue Carol Shalley

The summer after graduating from UC Boulder with a degree in Spanish, I loaded my un-air-conditioned Volkswagen Bug with all my possessions and set off to visit friends and look for a job speaking Spanish.

My family questioned why I was leaving Colorado, my birthplace and home, especially without a job. I was ready for adventure and opportunities—that was my dream, my "WHY."

The day I departed, my grandmother gave me a cooler, a block of ice, and a paper fan, and told me, "That's how we air-conditioned our cars when I was young." They didn't cool anything, but no matter—I was on my way!

By the time I arrived in Houston, Texas, I was almost out of money. I was hired as a secretary despite my weak typing skills, and I was fired after one week. I was not going home! No matter how challenging, I was resolute to not go back.

I went to the library every day (an intuitive nudge), rented a manual typewriter for twenty-five cents an hour, and practiced diligently. My determination paid off, and I won a new job working in Mexico. My dream came true!

- Be clear about "WHY" you are selling your product or taking action. When you believe with total conviction that your offering is sacred, that it serves you and others, obstacles will not deter you.
- Your "WHY" may change over time, but you can create prosperity, love, and purpose— whatever you want—when you believe unconditionally in your "WHY," set goals, and go after them.

Sales Is the Exchange of Divine Energy and Love

At times I doubted whether selling my services was worthwhile. Was it mercenary or inconsequential compared to authors, philanthropists, and speakers who touch and transform millions of lives?

- Making money, selling products, providing services, creating jobs, paying for goods, or giving to others is an exchange of blessed energy.

When I first started selling, I would blast potential customers with the features and benefits of my products. If I made enough calls and presentations, I would win sales and reach my income goals, but meaningful connections and relationships were missing.

I also learned that selling is serving your customers by providing the best product or service that meets their needs, makes their jobs and lives easier, cares for them, and listens to them. Every person wants to tell their story and be heard.

- You are their advocate and helpful partner, finding the feeling and dreams behind their purchase and genuinely communicating that you see their magnificence. By noticing details about them, a splendid exchange is created. Trust and community will grow and expand.
- When you sell with kindness, optimism, and gratitude, you increase the powerful energy of opportunities and love. What is glorious is that it's a two-way exchange. You also earn the energy of money, and your value is recognized.

The "Magic"

Twenty years ago, I was fired from a cool marketing job. A week later my mother died of cancer. At first, I felt lost and couldn't see my "what's next." As I began to investigate possibilities, I knew I should own a company since being an employee wasn't my strongest skill. My husband had a part-time business conducting architectural surveys. My intuition flashed—why not market his business? Because it was operating, I would have to research and dream how to grow it.

I went to the library every week and read the classified ads from large cities looking for companies seeking field architects. If they were hiring, perhaps they would outsource architectural services. I identified hiring managers, cold-called them, and was rejected by many, but I kept going. Then I sent our information with something I hoped would get their attention: empty paint cans filled with cookies.

To differentiate our outreach, I thought about what I loved to do, and what people appreciated: baking. Perhaps sending cookies was not "corporate," but I love nourishing people with homemade items. Cookies in paint cans generated many responses, and Jack in the Box and Exxon Mobil were our first new clients.

• We all have "Magic"—it is doing what we love and what attracts people to us.

Your "Magic" may be creative thinking or having great vision. Maybe it's writing, crafting beautiful things, or storytelling. Perhaps you make people laugh, can develop fortuitous relationships, or are an expert at social media.

• When you combine your "Magic" with your "Why" and come from love and desire to serve, you propel yourself forward. The need for outside validation diminishes. It becomes easier to keep going even if your product doesn't resonate with every potential client. Hold on to what makes you and your product special and be confident that there are people who are a match for your sacred offerings.

Have a Party!

Every time someone selects my service or product, I stop and have a party. I revel when the sale isn't realized too.

Celebrate yourself for being brave enough to ask for presentations and sales, doing things that might make you uncomfortable, not allowing unease or fear to diminish your "Why" and "Magic," and staying steadfast, knowing the right clients will come to you.

Getting a "no" isn't failure. It could be that the potential client is having a sad day and their "no" has nothing to do with you. And a "no" is the opportunity to retool and practice.

Sales is a series of small wins. Cheer as the process develops—your research or networking identifies the user of your product, you find the decision maker, you make the call, you send an email, you book an appointment, and you take the time to hear what the client wants. Be persistent; these steps add up to the sale.

There are days when the thought of asking is overwhelming, and my energy is drab. Then I hear my mother's voice telling me, "Say thank you."

- Gratitude raises your energy and vibration. It opens the connection to new possibilities and the people who are looking for you. Stay in grateful, celebratory energy before the sale is made, claiming it as if it's already happened.
- To wonder if you're off track when you don't get responses from the selling steps is normal. Don't give up! The flow of grateful energy will bring unforeseen wins, such as being referred to the right client by the prospect who wasn't interested.

Pop the cork—you rock!

"More, Please" (*Más, Por Favor*)

Recently, my company had $320,000 in receivables but not enough cash to make payroll. I was so distressed.

I had been listening to a book, *Love Money, Money Loves You,* by Sarah McCrum. She writes about feeling destitute when her business failed, and then Money channeled her. On my freak-out day, I was listening to a chapter where Money says, "When you ask for more money, we give you more money, but we also give you more bills."

That was an AHA! I realized that the energy I was putting out was lack and fear, and I noticed how many times I desperately said, "I need more money." With a flash of understanding and intuition, I rephrased my requests to "Thank you for the money in" (for completed work), "Thank you for the money out" (paying our bills), and "More, Please!"

With delight and gratitude, we received payments to make payroll then and ever since, and our annual sales have increased to over three million dollars.

"More, Please" is the tool that shifts my vibration and the way I go forward. It is a combination of being grateful for what is now, opening myself to the belief I am worthy of abundance, asking for what I want, and knowing with absolute certainty that "More, Please" will come to me.

- Find your own "More Please" to keep you in the positive energy of love, giving, and receiving.

Fun and Ease

We are meant to prosper with ease, play, and fun. The Universe gives us intuitive sparkles and moments of inspiration to live our "Why." It does not want us to stress, doubt our value, or work millions of hours.

If we don't like the steps to achieve a goal, we're not likely to reach it. When we create a way to make those tasks enjoyable, we will realize the goal.

Adding nuggets of pleasure and party-energy as you complete your selling steps will increase your vibration so you will make more sales, increase your revenue, and have fun along the journey.

The Universe wants us to make time to pet the dog, call a friend, go for a walk, look at silly YouTube videos, dance to "Wooly Bully," and plan your post-COVID adventure.

- "Use your feelings of enjoyment as your compass, guiding you infallibly towards a bright future." —*Love Money, Money Loves You*

When you create your offering, ask, "How do I want my business to show up?" People want to dream, and you can be a compassionate change maker to meet their needs and wishes, spreading grace, love, and delight.

- Always remember that when you dream, act, and let go of the how things will be realized, you are the vibration of infinite possibilities, opportunities, and your own prosperity.

Rock on!

Sue Carol Shalley is passionate about coaching entrepreneurs to vanquish their fear of asking for business. She has a successful track record in business development and marketing and has created a multimillion-dollar business whose clientele is Fortune 500 companies.

Her sales training programs are lively, fun, and proven to increase revenue.

www.ProsperKindly.com

29. IT REALLY DOES TAKE A VILLAGE

Karen Strauss

Barely glancing at me, the technician told me to go back to the waiting room as they needed to get more pictures of me. When you have had as many mammograms as I have, I knew what that meant.

I sat and waited, sat and waited some more . . . I was petrified, anguished, paralyzed. I kept going up to the front desk and asking when they would call me back. I waited another thirty minutes, and finally I could not breathe—my adrenaline was pumping and I thought I was going to faint.

So I ran! Out of the double doors—out into the street where the sun was shining that warm July day. I ran to the bus to take me home so I could put my head under the covers, irrationally thinking that if the words weren't spoken, I wouldn't have the dreaded "c" word.

On the bus my cell phone kept ringing. When I got home, the phone was still ringing. I had several messages from the lab telling me it was urgent I go back.

I finally called them and scheduled my appointment for the next morning at 8:00 a.m. Next I called my best friend. She dropped everything and listened and then insisted that she go with me the next day. It didn't hurt that she is a women's health provider and knows her way around an X-ray.

They confirmed that I had breast cancer. The bad news was that it had already started to spread outside the duct, but the cancer was really small, and it had been caught early.

I will never forget the walk home, with my friend Susan holding my hand. She said, "You are going to be fine. It will be a rough journey for a while, but you will be just fine. You will come to see this as just a bump in the road."

Well, I am not going to lie. It felt like much more than a bump in the road during that long, dreadful year, but during that time I realized how many amazing friends and supporters I had.

The biopsy, endless meetings with surgeons, oncologists, my primary doctor . . . Susan was with me through all of it. I was so grateful to her; she was my advocate. She took notes; she could hear what the doctors were saying, while I could barely listen.

Finally we found the right team. I had the surgery—I needed a mastectomy. I woke up in the hospital to four worried faces trying to put on a brave front: my family, Susan, my cousin . . .

Everybody said at once, "It went great!" That was the beginning of my transformation, although I didn't know it yet.

You see, I had always been a very independent woman. Even when I was very young, I could always "do it myself." I didn't need anyone to help me; *I* was the one who people turned to when they needed to talk about their problems. I always saw needing help from someone as weak. I was the strong one. I was not going to be vulnerable—I would manage just fine! I could take care of managing my business, my clients, my employees, my co-op, my house in the country, my dog—and now my cancer. This was just one more thing . . . right?

Well, I could not have been more wrong! I didn't realize what a big deal this was, and I needed to focus every bit of attention on getting well. From choosing the surgeon, the oncologist, getting second and third opinions to finally undergoing the surgery, enduring more endless tests, and setting up the chemo treatment. And then living with the effects of the chemo itself—the nausea, the fatigue, the memory loss . . .

Throughout this process, I don't know how I would have made it through without my family, good friends—and surprisingly even those that weren't such good friends. For instance, one person (now an Oscar winner for the movie *Birdland*!) whom I knew from the dog park called me and offered to take my dog, Izzy, to the park anytime I wanted. I did not know him very well at that point, and his generous offer floored me.

Similar offers came. A woman in my building is a makeup artist, and when I had a swanky holiday party to attend, she offered to do my makeup—complete with false eyelashes! And one night, when I decided it was time to cut the remaining hair on my head (a very emotional decision for me), my friend (whose husband works on Broadway) brought over one of her friends who cuts hair professionally for Broadway productions. They made it fun—we had champagne and hors d'oeuvres.

One neighbor, whom I knew just to say hello to, came to my apartment every night while I was going through chemo to check on me, see if I needed anything, and offer to walk Izzy. This was a lifesaver, since by then I was pretty wiped out and sometimes couldn't even make it off the couch, let alone get dressed in five layers, dress Izzy, and walk outside in 10 degree weather so Izzy could do his business.

I could go on and on about the generosity and support offered to me by friends, family, and acquaintances who were ready and willing to do something, anything, to help me. And for the first time in my life, I let them! Wow! What a feeling—I went from feeling guilty to feeling grateful and appreciative of the fact that so many people wanted to support and help me. All I had to do was say yes and give them a task.

So many people came to sit with me during the four hours each week I had my chemo treatment. My friends who thought they were stand-up comedians practiced on me, their captive audience. Some of my friends came to gossip, or spill their problems, or just discuss world events. I was SO grateful not to have to talk about "how I was feeling," or about my illness in general. It made the time fly by.

I have never forgotten this lesson. I no longer want to be a loner, to have to make decisions by myself, to not allow myself to be vulnerable. This has stood me in good stead to grow my business as well as become more intimate in my personal relationships.

I've learned that life is more fun when I let people in. I no longer feel the weight of the world on my shoulders. I know I have mentors, friends, advisors, and loved ones who will keep me grounded, supported, and constantly aware that I do not have to go through life alone.

It really does take a village—and I am deeply and profoundly grateful!

Karen Strauss is a speaker, book coach, and author, with more than thirty-five years in the publishing industry. As the founder of Hybrid Global Publishing, she works with speakers, authors, and entrepreneurs to write, publish, distribute, and promote their books in order to generate unlimited leads, get on more speaking stages, and grow their business by attracting more clients.

www.HybridGlobalPublishing.com

30. THE EMERGENCE OF AN ART COLLECTIVE

Tom Franco

Being a visual artist is an unforgiving task. Pretty much on day one, an artist is thrust into the deep end of discovery, and everything is out in the open for others to see. It is both equally rewarding and challenging.

At the age of twenty-two, my life was full of yearning for "How do I do it?"

The bitter paradox that struck me square in the face was that coming out of art school with a full degree was not going to pay even 1 percent of the bills.

I did what I was told with a sincerity and belief in an outcome for sixteen years of my youth, only to wind up confused and tired and on a hunt for God only knows what. I turned to spirituality for answers. I gave up art completely for one year, but that ended with depression and anxiety. I looked for older and professional role models, but no one seemed to have a complete answer for how to be an artist.

One year later, in 2003, I moved to Oakland, California, to finish my last attempt at art school and figure out who could help me. I took one class at a time and worked three jobs, mostly in the area of childcare, male nanny by day. I also taught meditation and art to families while living in a local ashram setting, my other outlet for grounding and positivity.

My desperation to make ends meet was high. In the school and ashram setting, I took away a few key lessons that stuck with me.

- **My personal schedule is dynamic;** it needs to change from day to day.
- **Keep learning new things,** especially when the tasks at hand seem pointless. A job learned well can instantly turn into a new job.
- **Work with the people already around me;** get out of my comfort zone and connect with creative people who interest me.
- **Visual art is not an isolated event;** always find new ways to break isolation.

At school I started doing collaborative projects with my classmates. We stayed up late at night goofing around and doing each other's homework.

I began a two-year phase of simply saying "yes" to anything that came my way, which brought me out of my rigid routines and into diverse groups of performers. I took tai chi and judo classes and competed in competitions, winning medals literally at my old high school where I never competed in anything before. I joined an avant-garde dance troupe with live musicians. We made original work every Sunday, and then performed all over the Bay Area and in Europe.

These were two highly dynamic environments that visual arts did not even come close to. So, I brought that collaborative vibe into the studio and challenged people to work side by side with me on the same piece, in clay. A few things came out of that.

- **I learned ten times faster.** We were sharing hands-on about the technical craft and showing off how to use the medium of clay.
- **I had so much more fun.** Suddenly art making was a performance with one or more people.
- **My selfish mind was ruined.** My desire to make the perfect piece, all by myself, dropped away. With a collaborator, my best ideas came flowing forth despite my judgments. It was a continual letting go of expectations.

These early days built a foundation on how to actually learn with a group. Rarely have I come across moments of pure collaboration like this, where the only rule is that everyone agrees equally when the piece is done. There is an inherent respect for one another built in. This has never gotten old and continues to motivate me in everything I do. It has led to my ultimate goal as an artist—being the person who makes my favorite works of art.

After art school, a handful of us continued the connection and opened our first art space in South Berkeley, California, with no safety net from established authorities. It was beyond anything I had ever come across in creative community. It became our own.

Creativity Is Expansion

One of my favorite teachers once said, "Have a clear vision of where you want to go in life, and then any decisions that come will either take you toward that vision or take you away from it."

You don't always have to do it by the book. There is such a thing called DIY—do it yourself!

Starting off, we had no budget, and a proper business plan would have killed the momentum. There was an excitement to just come together as artists—we didn't even need a physical location; we were just planting seed ideas. Then it became clear that a location would give us legitimacy.

I had a dream one night of a homeless man who managed a building by collecting rent while living in the bushes. He spoke to me about staying out of sight, how there is a time and place for being "underground." That was how we started, out of the public eye. The Firehouse Art Collective was born.

The first location was an old 1800s fire station with three stories—two big art studios on the ground floor and two floors of apartments. It was a dump. We started with baby steps and needed at least eight people to rent a part of the studios for around $275 per month each. I called everyone I could think of to join us—even old friends from kindergarten!

With sheer adrenaline, we took the plunge. Whatever we could demolish or build ourselves, we did, or we negotiated with the landlord. A baseline mutual respect with the owners developed that lasted ten years.

I refer to those first two years as my most prolific time making art. I went over to the studio at night after work and spent an hour or two painting or working on my sculptures, and the other members would show up on their own schedules. Even if I just came in exhausted for ten minutes to blankly stare at my work, that was enough.

We started with three volunteer managers. My specialty role was to never stop meeting new artists. Two truths emerged that proved our business sustainable.

- **There are always artists out there.** They are ready to go to great lengths in order to make their art and have a space to do it. Whether they know it or not, they need community.
- **In a shared studio, with twenty-four-hour access, it never gets crowded.** People come in on their own time, and it naturally balances itself out.

After expanding to both studios downstairs with sixteen people, we decided to take over the apartments upstairs because we had too many artists moving away. Having the artists live on-site was a bigger investment in our people. The first year of co-living was like having thirteen new best friends. Everyone was super excited. People wouldn't even go out on the weekend; they would all just hang out together or go to events together. We became a one-stop shop for the artist experience.

Yet the collective community was not all fun and games. Every single person was put to the test to be their most authentic self. There was truly a self-editing process in that if someone didn't get along with group dynamics, they would usually decide to leave. Conflict resolution became a real skill, and we had to formalize our building rules and our expectations of one another. Power is a drug, and each manager had to be a living example for the others.

After four years of sweat and fun, the group decided that we should start a second location as a gallery to show off the art. Having backyard art shows and open studio events, with special themes and workshops was great, but we needed to be more professional. We once again took over a new location with a communal group in charge.

This kind of forward momentum continued for the first eight years. Our peak expansion was six fully functioning spaces with around one hundred renting artists, and hundreds more interacting with us. We had seven small galleries with art openings every month. Some artists made a career out of their time with us, such as incubating cafes and always, someone's very first art show!

Today, in 2020, the Firehouse Art Collective has been going for sixteen years. Some spaces have come and gone due to leases ending or buildings being sold. My current motto is: "Make your art! And don't operate the spaces by yourself."

My wife and business partner, Iris Franco, is a film producer, and together we established *Firehouse Films*. We make features and documentaries that highlight the artist's role in communities with the goal of reaching a broader audience.

I also invite a small group of my favorite artistic collaborators around the US and other countries to do invitational art shows, murals, and installations at different galleries, museums, and festivals. We absolutely love coming to a location and making art on-site in the vibe of the local community.

Our financial model is ripe for investors to amplify this work. Ultimately, the Firehouse Art Collective pays for itself, and this kind of art and community model is able to thrive in any city. We have a franchise-model trademark that is ready for expansion.

Community Is the Means

Being an artist is the practice of creating things *and* engaging in community. How do you share your creations? Or is the system for sharing nonexistent? Don't wait for someone to save you or promote you—be an active part of your own community. A group of people working together is a much stronger promotional tool than one artist working alone.

Pure collaboration moments are exhilarating—any activity that gets you in the zone of peak performance with others. This is the true essence of collaboration. You can apply art to all types of human-run structures and organization. Lead with the creative arts, and you can infuse art into people's daily lives for positive results.

Firehouse Art Collective serves the whole artist. We embrace all aspects of living a truly creative life. The role of the artist in society is a big one. The artist is a community leader with a beautiful voice and guides us to where we are going next. Some people call this culture.

Think big, take chances, love what you do, adjust as needed, stay healthy, love people, and have fun!

Tom Franco is a visual artist, community builder, culture influencer, and film producer—in that order. He lives and works in California. Tom directs a constellation of physical locations called the Firehouse Art Collective, which provides community settings for art studios, co-living, event space and, retail for the arts.

www.FirehouseArtCollective.com

31. PLAYING A BIGGER GAME

Natalie Ledwell

We had temporarily moved from Australia, our native country, to the US, basically surviving on credit cards for the five months before launching Mind Movies in September 2008. Of course, that's when the economic crisis hit the planet and we'd already racked up $120,000 in debt.

To say "If this thing doesn't work, we will be toast!" was an understatement.

It would take too long to go through everything that went wrong with that launch, but clearly we did a few things right. We ended up doing a $700,000 launch!

Yes, $700,000 on our first launch—and our product cost ONLY $97. Our email list went from 8,000 to 80,000 subscribers in one week!

As you can imagine, that really put us on the map. But if you look at the game that we're playing now, our email list is around a million subscribers, give or take. We've reached nearly six million people around the world. Our annual revenue this year is on target to reach eight figures!

It's a bigger game that we're playing.

My company is called Mind Movies. A Mind Movie is the digital version of a vision board. It's a combination of affirmations, photos, and music. My main product is actually video creation software for you to create your own vision of your life and future. Inside the software, there's a whole library of affirmations and photos and music—all royalty free—that you can use, or you can use your own photos and music. Once you've created your digital vision board, you can then download it to your device and carry it around. It's a very effective visualization tool.

When you're visualizing to create something in your life eliciting the law of attraction, not only do you need to be able to see it very vividly as a movie in your mind, you also need to be able to feel what it's like to already be there. The addition of music is the secret sauce. If you choose the right song that absolutely blows your hair back, that song becomes an anchor for you; it becomes the soundtrack for your vision.

For my original Mind Movie, back in 2006, I used Coldplay's "Clocks." To this day, every time that song comes on the radio, I'm easily brought to tears because it was the beginning of *everything*.

When we started Mind Movies, Glen, my husband then, could hardly turn on a computer. I knew nothing about computers or the internet. I only used my computer for bookkeeping. And we started from there.

We had a small email list, but it was very responsive. We were doing video sales letters before we even knew what we were on to. It was just something we kind of fell into. Because people would see us on video, they warmed up to us. It was a big part of our success.

Then we started getting emails from people saying, "This is changing my life." I told Glen and our business partner Ryan, "We have to get serious about this. This is changing people's lives. This isn't a hobby anymore. This isn't something just on the side."

There are a few major factors that I believe really helped in our success.

First, the smartest thing we did was to join internet marketing legend Frank Kern's mastermind group. At Frank's big live event, we were invited to apply to join his private mastermind. While I was excitedly filling out the application as to why he should accept us, Glen and Ryan were sitting next to me saying, "Should we do this? Will we actually get access to him? Is it going to be worth it?"

It was a $2,700-a-month commitment that we didn't have because we were living on credit cards. I just got up and started walking away, and Glen asked, "What are you doing?"

I replied, "Hey, this is why we're here. I know it doesn't look like we can afford it, but we will work it out." We were accepted into the mastermind, and of course, I took full credit.

Joining that mastermind group and surrounding ourselves with the right people that could give us the right advice and the right support at the right time took our game to the next level!

The other thing that helped us step into this bigger game was knowing from the beginning our VISION of what the company would look like.

Glen, who is now my ex-husband/business partner, said, "OK, this is the lifestyle we want, so let's reverse-engineer from there to see what kind of business we can set up that's going to help us live that lifestyle."

It starts with becoming a "Vibrational Match."

Living in San Diego while working on the launch, when we were fully stressed, we would leave our apartment, where we were working up to twelve hours a day, and sit at the Dog Beach. Watching dogs frolicking on the beach helped us to raise our frequency.

From that higher frequency, we had conversations, in present tense, as if the launch were already a massive success. I talked about how we were only working six hours a day and all the things we were doing with our families. We also talked about the team we were building. We would *feel* what it was like to already be there.

Today, our team in San Diego manages all the satellite teams. We have a team of programmers and app builders in Lithuania. We also have a team in the Philippines, consisting of our video editors, customer support, and social media.

Having "the right team" around us is another essential element of our success.

So if you're looking at where you are now and thinking, *Well, I need to take a quantum leap into this bigger place,* think about what changes you want to make for your team. What changes do you want to make to the structure of your business?

If you want the "Freedom Lifestyle" or you just want to play a bigger game, make sure you have the right team around you.

There's always another level to play a BIGGER game!

About six years ago, I started hearing this little voice saying, "Natalie, you're wasting time."

"What do you mean I'm wasting time?" I would say to that little voice. "Look at everything I'm doing and all the changes I'm making. We're making the world a better place. Look how big this is. I don't understand what you mean."

That was the same little voice that I heard about a year before my marriage ended. By that time it was already gone. We just reached the end. And honestly, we have a fantastic relationship to this day. "Not over, just different" is the term I coined when we separated.

We're still business partners. We're still good friends. Our relationship has just transitioned into something different. We still love and respect each other.

While it was a great marriage, by the time we got toward the end, I realized that I was blaming him for so many things. *I can't shine because he's the man, and he's got to be the front person. It's his fault that I can't step into my greatness.*

Of course, when our marriage ended, I lost my scapegoat. I knew if I didn't step up and do whatever it was that was calling me, I'd have only myself to blame.

I remember the first week after we broke up. In my newfound freedom, as a single woman, my whole question was, "Oh my God, who am I without him?" We had been together for twenty years. We were one of those couples that everyone knew. Suddenly it was "I have no identity without him."

About four days later, my perspective shifted to "Wait, who do I *want* to be? I have a platform. I don't have to worry about money. I have a successful business. I can live anywhere I want." So I went to work. I enrolled in the Hoffman Process. I was committed to discovering what my contribution to the end of my marriage was. In trying to figure out what the next thing was going to be, I said yes to *everything*.

In my personal Mind Movie, I wanted to launch a TV show and write another book. I had created twelve personal growth lessons for kids, but I didn't know what to do with them. I realized that I hadn't really made any progress with these things. And, to be really honest, I probably had carried them over from the year before.

I knew I needed to focus on ONE thing. I said to myself, "Well, it won't be the kids program because I'm not qualified. I don't know what to do with that. It's not in my wheelhouse. It's just too hard."

Then I said, "The TV show—now that's sexy. That's what I want to do . . . or write another book. I want to do one of these two things." But I realized that was my ego talking.

Two days later, I was having a conversation with my colleague, Debbie Seldon, who has worked with kids in trauma for fifteen years and has earned two master's degrees. She said, "I need to do this curriculum with you. We need to help this next generation of kids coming through."

Oh, I thought, *it's gonna be the kids program. I never would have guessed.* I realized that when I started talking with her, something inside of me shifted. I knew this was what I was meant to do and where I needed to focus.

Now, very similar to how unqualified we were when we started Mind Movies, I felt just as unqualified to work with kids on personal growth.

I left school when I was fifteen years old. Back then in Australia, you could leave high school at the end of tenth grade. Even though I was smart enough to carry on, being from a very big family of eight kids, Mom and Dad couldn't afford to keep me at school.

The other thing was that I didn't have kids. My small self came up with all the reasons and all the excuses why I should not be doing this. "I'm not qualified—who do I think I am? Seriously, education?" I remember having a little meltdown. At one point I said, "I can't do this. I'm not the person for this."

I have a little process that helps me move through those moments when my small self is telling me, "You can't do it; you're not qualified . . . who do you think you are?"

As I sit in meditation, I go to the end result. I'm not looking at the lifestyle this time; I already have that. I'm looking at the result that I'm actually creating. If you just say, "I want to be successful," well, that can mean a million different things. So just choose one moment or one scene that represents what you desire. When you go into visualization, rather than seeing yourself as a character in a movie, actually put yourself in the center. Use all of your senses.

When I do this visualization, I actually put myself in a classroom in Liberia, Africa, the first country to invite our program into their schools. Liberia is still reeling with PTSD, as they've only been out of civil war for six years. Their people are feeling defeated, as if there's no future and no hope.

Sitting quietly with my eyes closed, I envision myself walking. I can hear the crunching of the gravel under my feet as I approach the classroom. It's hot, and I'm swatting flies away, but then as I walk into the classroom, I can feel it getting cooler, because the roof is there. It's cooler on my skin. Then I can hear the kids. They're screaming and running up to me, pulling on my clothes. I'm trying to get to the teachers. The kids all have these huge smiles on their faces, and the teachers are crying with gratitude for how much of a difference our program has made in their lives.

When I sit in that visualization, I'm hearing, tasting, feeling, and touching everything that's going on. I create that event on a daily basis, at least once and preferably multiple times. That visualization process shifts my energy from self-doubt into a frequency of gratitude. Feeling gratitude opens me to receive and gives me the confidence to fully own my own greatness.

Stepping into the arena of this bigger game, I have a lot of people telling me how difficult it is to get into the school system because of all the red tape. I can't listen to that. I've chosen not to listen to the people that are saying it can't be done, because that stops me from moving forward. I know my ability to manifest.

We've built a platform to deliver this kids program with over 280 lessons, including twenty lessons per grade, from K–12. The teachers just have to play a video or read the dialogue, and then they can teach the class.

We've also created an under-twelves version of the Mind Movies software and a teenage version with photos and life areas that are age-specific. All the kids get access to Mind Movies, so they can make their own digital vision boards as well.

We're looking at how we support the teachers. What can we do to give them the support that they need?

The teachers will have free access to online coaching programs, so they can create, manifest, and get rid of the challenges and the blocks they have in their own lives.

We're not teaching law of attraction. This is all psychology and science-based. We're looking at things like empathy, compassion, self-esteem, and the sense of belonging.

We want to put all of these skills and tools in the hands of children. We can give them the structure to build their self-esteem and to encourage them to think outside of the box, to be able to come up with these solutions to address their most critical challenges. I can't wait to see what they create.

Imagine what's possible by bringing these personal growth strategies to children around the world!

Aussie **Natalie Ledwell** is an internationally renowned motivational speaker, bestselling author, host of *The Inspiration Show* and *Wake Up TV!* and co-founder of the revolutionary personal development company Mind Movies. Her mission is to empower ten million adults and kids all over the world to lead lives fulfilled with joy, happiness, and passion.

MindMovies.com

32. AWAKENING TO EXPONENTIAL MOMENTUM IN LOVE, LIFE, AND BUSINESS

Lars Rain Gustafsson

The awakening to momentum is a spectacular unfolding of awareness that we live in a continuous flow of magical infinite energy.

So how can we can move this magical infinite energy, direct it, accelerate it, or even potentially block it?

In the end we are always creating momentum that either expands our love, relationships, business, income, and life experience, or hurtles us into significant challenges.

This continuous magical infinite energy is the secret elixir of life.

When we are in the flow state, we expand our awareness into our true infinite nature.

All of life aligns with the current that momentum creates.

When we honor and fully embrace this flow, it's as if we unlock a part of us that is elevated to have the capacity to handle the synchronicities we experience from the magical flow.

The key to creating and handling momentum in any area of our lives is building our capacity.

This capacity for momentum is an awareness I have observed thousands of times that aligns with the life lesson that "you will only be challenged equal and proportionate to what you can handle, and a little bit more."

This is either good news or not, depending on your vantage point from within a challenge and how much it is affecting your life. I have observed this within teams, cities, and even nations. Think about the dramatic state of the world in 2020. The good news is that those of us who are aware and take care of ourselves and others can handle the sheer momentum of all the outcomes of this year because we have created the capacity of love to handle these tumultuous times.

Ever since learning this lesson about only being given what I could handle and a "little bit more" twenty years ago, I began a quest to build my capacity, which led to many discoveries in health, beliefs, spiritual and consciousness rituals, and habits. The most significant ritual I learned for building capacity is to practice detachment so that I am not emotionally engaged in the challenges in any situation. In other words, being in the observer mode 24/7, and operating from my heart.

So the ultimate key to tapping into the momentum of an infinite flow of magic and miracles is the ability to be detached.

Becoming aware of momentum in every area of life—from relationships to growing your business—is an awakening to the subtle ways in which every thought, action, and nonaction influences a faster and more magnified flow of the universal magical energy through and around you.

You have always been creating momentum, whether positive or negative. These are also only perceptions, depending on your vantage point. You are either blocking energy flow to create positive momentum, or you are being in your full power and directing the energy flow to create the life of your dreams.

Realize that once you become aware of momentum and start to actively direct your energy from an unattached perspective, it will affect every other area of your life. Momentum in business will, for instance, require momentum in your health, relationships, personal growth, and spiritual capacity.

Five years into my quest to grow my capacity and handle more, I met a life coach who taught me a three-step process I could use to completely let go of all attachments and return to my inner infinite power. All interactions in life create a psychic bond, an energetic chord, so to speak. These draw on our energy at a conscious and unconscious level, constantly limiting our ability to move forward with greater momentum and handle more in life. These chords are like millions of little strings that hold us down. The more attached we are, the more we form a ceiling on our results in all areas of life.

Did I get sidetracked over the years and forget to practice this detachment process?

Yes, absolutely!

The more I struggled with challenges, the more attached I became, and therefore the less I could handle.

Remember, the Universe only challenges you "equal and proportionate to what you can handle, and a little bit more." In my case it continuously felt like I had a ceiling in my business and life. No matter how hard I tried, I couldn't bust through this ceiling.

Then, in the early part of 2019, I was reminded about this detachment process by my life coach and spiritual guide, Ed Strachar, and I began to make this the number-one ritual in my spiritual practice. From the moment I started practicing these detachment steps from morning to night, my entire reality shifted into the purest and most delicious flow state. What was not in tune with this new level of energy I was achieving daily either shifted (transmuted) or dropped away. Some of those dynamics were quite painful, as I was very attached to some people and certain aspects of the way I thought things should be, but in the end, it resulted in a magnitude of gains and momentum in all aspects of my life and business.

Here is the full detachment process that Ed sent me (shared with his permission) that will help you to regain your full power as an infinite being, free of all attachments and chords in your life. I suggest going through this process as often as you can every day.

****

Detach from all attachments except heaven and earth.

Getting out of your head and quieting your mind is very important to center yourself in your power, a state from which pure detachment is possible.

To quiet your mind is simple: Just use your breath and your heartbeat.

Breathe deeply and hold for fifteen heartbeats (if fifteen is hard, do less. If fifteen is easy, do more; it should be a stretch but not a strain). Still your mind and exhale very slowly through your mouth . . . then hold for three heartbeats.

While doing this, concentrate your mental energy in the center of your head. This is key. Still your mind and increase your strength at the same time.

Do three or more cycles of this as often as needed. (Do it with a smile.)

Repeat for three cycles and continuously increase to seventeen and four . . . twenty and five, etc. When you are able to, stretch further and increase your strength, willpower, and inner peace.

While high in vibration in your energy body, see each issue and person in your life as a tethered balloon tied to your body with a wire, draining some of your life force.

Then detach and feel the drain stop by cutting it with a pair of spiritual scissors.

Then—from your heart—command and demand(!) and recall all your power to return three times.

Then demand and command(!) that all energies that are not yours, as well as all attachments that do not serve your highest good, detach and leave forever.

In doing this, feel a rush of light from the heavens come and "bathe" you and take all down into mother earth.

****

When you are done, you will have a visceral, cellular, and full energetic experience of being whole, perfect, and complete. A peace that surpasses all understanding will fill your whole being. I suggest practicing this at least three to five times a day until it becomes innate and instant anytime you let your energy get "hooked" into any person or experience.

Within this new state, you will begin to live and experience life from a completely new perspective, completely free of all attachments. At first some attachments will come back very quickly, but with time, you will release these as well. Things toward which you had a negative charge will quickly melt away and transform into a new, loving, and compassionate perspective.

A new resonance will fill every aspect of your life. You will literally see things with "new eyes" and attract into your life what you have always wanted. You will be a self-referential being, able to discern the truth in any situation and no longer attached to what that is. Truth can be painful or liberating, depending on your attachment to the way you think things need to be.

All attachments drain your energy. By cutting these chords and calling back all your power and releasing what is not yours, you enter into a state of pure being-ness. Your life force returns to its full power. Your intuition is completely turned on, and you are not drained by others or your perceptions of them. More truth will be revealed to you—equal and proportionate to how you handle it, and a little bit more.

Life is love and can be experienced as pure energy. The momentum that will start to happen in your relationships, personal growth, income, and business will now be proportionate to what you can handle, and a little bit more. The more you practice detachment, the more the magic flow will envelop you, guide you, and support you in all your visions and goals.

Life is all about experiencing the infinite energy that we are as we participate in directing our total power to creating heaven on earth.

Bio
Lars Rain Gustafsson, founder of the BodyMind Institute (established in 2009) and UEXL Institute (established in 2017), is a passionate purveyor and developer of advanced health, life, business, and personal development education. With momentum, community, networking, and education systems in place, Lars now has his sights set on supporting and creating a worldwide revolution in online education.
www.uexl.org

33. VISION, VALUES, AND VELOCITY

Nancy Matthews

It's interesting, even somewhat unbelievable, to me that a young girl who was picked on, riddled with low self-esteem, and never felt like she fit in is now the leader of a worldwide organization that has served thousands of women. In 2008, through a strange series of twists and turns, I founded Women's Prosperity Network with my two sisters (yes, my actual sisters—same mom and dad, growing up together in Brooklyn, New York).

We created what we now recognize as a "Soul Tribe": a community of like-minded and like-spirited women (and some extraordinary men too) who are committed to making a positive impact in the world. Looking back, it is easy to trace the steps (and some of the missteps) we have taken to build our community. The specific steps and strategies have changed along the way, but what has never changed is the culture of our community and who we are as leaders.

You've probably heard the phrase "The speed of the leader determines the speed of the pack," and I would venture to say that it is the vision, values, and then the velocity of the leader that determines the soul of a tribe.

Vision

From the first moment we shared the vision for Women's Prosperity Network, women joined us, saying, "Yes, yes, yes!" It was as though our words contained a magnetic force that attracted just the right people to us. While the words we shared were important, and we spent days crafting our message, it was the **essence** behind those words that created the magnetic force.

Vision in this context is the ability to see into the future, tapping into your soul and your heart's desires, and then visioning the intended result through your mind's eye. It is the ability to believe without seeing in physical form a desired result, outcome, or impact. To create a vision that is infused with the essence of your purpose and your passion, consider the following:

- What is the end result you want to create?
- How do you want to see the world (or group of people, condition, or circumstance) transformed as the result of the work you do?

Here are some examples to inspire you as you create your vision statement:

Women's Prosperity Network:
A world of impassioned, determined women who honor themselves and one another and work together as a massive force for positive change in the world

Author and Publisher (who writes stories about "courage under siege"):
A world where people treat each other with compassion and empathy

Accountant:
A world where business owners thrive as they bring their products and services to others

Money Mindset Coach:
A world where people bathe themselves in self-compassion and easily receive the abundance available to them

A well-developed vision statement makes it easy for those who have a shared vision to find and connect with you so that you can then co-create the desired impact through their unique contribution to the vision.

Seth Godin, the author of *Tribes*, defines a tribe as follows: "A tribe is a group of people connected to one another, connected to a leader and connected to an idea." He then goes on to say, "The secret of leadership is simple: do what you believe in. Paint a picture of the future. Go there. People will follow."

Creating a vision statement infused with your purpose, passion, and soul calling paints that picture.

Values

Values: A person's principles or standards of behavior;
one's judgment of what is important in life. (Oxford Dictionary)

Once you cast your vision and your soul tribe begins to gather the key components, keeping them connected to the vision lies in who you are as a leader and the values you live by and demonstrate.

Values are the basis of your code of ethics and your manner of operation (both personally and professionally). They are the rules by which you live and reflect what is most important to you. Living by your values serves as a navigational map to guide you in the decision making that keeps you in alignment with your vision.

After creating the vision for what we wanted Women's Prosperity Network to achieve, we then asked ourselves, "If that is our vision, who do we need to be? What do we stand for? What do we value?"

Here are the values we defined and continue to live and lead by:

- A heart-centered core; people before profits
- Impeccable communication

- Coop-etition instead of competition
- Honesty and integrity
- Kaizen—continuous improvement; we are mentored and we mentor others
- An abundance mentality
- Faith instead of fear

As a bonus, we found a quote that sums up the essence of our vision and our values and also serves as one of our mantras: "We may not have it all together, but together we have it all" (author unknown).

As your tribe grows and expands, you will have countless opportunities to use your values as the standard by which you make decisions. Knowing your values will serve you at every turn and make it easier for your tribe to stand by you, even when you take some missteps.

Several years ago we partnered with a coaching company to support us in delivering a next-level coaching program to our community. We did what we believed to be ample due diligence before agreeing to the joint venture, asked all the right questions (and were given all the "right" answers), and moved forward with the venture.

Unfortunately, the answers we were given as to this company's values, priorities, and manner of doing business were not actually carried out in their actions. This was a big misstep that created massive dissention among our tribe and difficulties for us in cleaning up the mess. What brought us through this potential fiasco was using our values as the guide for how we would handle the situation.

- **People before profits.** We personally delivered the services promised or refunded monies paid to anyone who was dissatisfied.
- **Impeccable communication.** Because our members knew that we wanted them to share their true experiences, it created the space for them to let us know what was not working so we could correct the situation.

- **Faith instead of fear.** We looked upon this misstep as an opportunity to create something even better for our own coaching program and believed that by staying true to our vision and our values, it would serve us rather than harm us.

Know your values and stand by them. As John Maxwell says, "A person's character is a person's best friend. It is the one thing you can count on when everything else goes to hell."

Velocity

As you seek to create and expand your soul tribe, you will absolutely want to stand out in a crowded marketplace, but it isn't necessarily the latest and greatest marketing strategies that will bring you the best results. Sure, you want to harness the power of those strategies and stay abreast of trends, but if your actions are not built upon the foundation of your vision and values, your efforts will fall short in producing the kind of results you truly desire.

Knowing and clearly communicating your vision and embodying that vision through your values are the essential predecessors to velocity: the speed at which you take action. After all, you wouldn't want to lead with massive speed in the wrong direction, would you?

In terms of velocity, what your soul tribe will most connect with and what will create the greatest amount of speed and growth are your "inspired actions." Let me explain.

We can take actions triggered by the fear of missing out, such as rushing into the marketplace without first having clearly defined your vision and values. We can take actions triggered by comparing ourselves to what others are doing, such as simply following the social media bandwagon over to the newest platform (even though your tribe may not be there.)

Or we can take actions that are inspired by our vision, enhanced by synchronicities that align with our vision, and supported by nature's flow and ease.

Inspired actions will always produce results because they are created from the depths of your soul and your heart's purest desires. Inspired actions tap into the spirit that resides in you—the essence from which all life comes forth—and in doing so, you easily connect with the spirit that resides in and through everything. This creates an almost magical force that signals the Universe to conspire in your favor so your actions bring about the desired results with greater ease and speed.

So how do you create a consistent flow of inspired actions that move you and your vision forward? This comes through a consistent practice of connecting with your soul (your spirit) and trusting your intuition. Through meditation and journaling, you are given the opportunity to become still so you can hear the small, still voice within. This is the voice of the Divine, speaking through you for the fulfillment of your unique purpose in this time and place. Following that voice with faith and commitment to your vision and values will provide the perfect velocity for you to lead, cultivate, and serve your soul tribe.

You have been called upon to lead at a time such as this.

You are perfectly prepared to step into your next level of expansion.

You are "The One" who has been tapped to make a positive impact in a way that only you can do.

Thank you for being "The One."

Nancy Matthews is a bestselling author, international speaker, Master NLP Practitioner, and master coach. She is the co-founder of Women's Prosperity Network, the author of *The One Philosophy: The Little Message with a BIG IMPACT* and *Visionaries with Guts,* and creator of the highly acclaimed *Receiving Your Riches* course.

www.NancyMatthews.com

NEXT STEPS

Soulful Leadership is about being clear in your stand while bringing people together to seek solutions for the common good.

Knowing who you want to BE often starts with knowing who you do NOT want to be and what you do not want to do.

A Soulful Leader does NOT . . .
Operate from Ego
Spew Hate
Act Selfishly
Practice "Power Over" Others
Lie, Cheat, or Steal
Seek to Harm Others
Surround Themselves with Cronies
Misinform
Manipulate
Disenfranchise
Segregate
Sacrifice People for Personal Gain

A Soulful Leader ...
Provides a Clear Vision in Alignment with Their Highest Truth
Takes Inspired Action
Seeks the Good of the Whole
Leads with Love and Compassion
Empowers Others through a Culture of "We"
Demonstrates Morality
Values Integrity and Honesty
Walks Their Talk
Keeps an Open Mind to New Ideas
Practices a Beginner's Mind—Always Eager to Learn
Collaborates Well with Others
Communicates Clearly
Appreciates Honest Feedback and Performance Review
Speaks and Listens from Their Heart
Honors Differences and Inspires Hope

If that sounds like you, YOUR leadership is needed!

Change is here now.
We have real work to do.

Complacency is no longer an option if we want to create a world of love together.

Leadership starts with you.
The choices you make every day really do matter.

Now is the time to step fully into your Soulful Leadership.

In addition to the treasures provided in each chapter, the authors have also provided special gifts to support your Hero's Journey. You can learn more about these authors and download their valuable tools at no cost by visiting our website, www.SoulfulLeadershipBook.com.

CPSIA information can be obtained
at www.ICGtesting.com
Printed in the USA
BVHW041640260121
598721BV00003B/7